interchange

FIFTH EDITION

T0306668

1

Workbook

Jack C. Richards
with Jonathan Hull and Susan Proctor

CAMBRIDGE
UNIVERSITY PRESS

CAMBRIDGE
UNIVERSITY PRESS & ASSESSMENT

Shaftesbury Road, Cambridge CB2 8EA, United Kingdom

One Liberty Plaza, 20th Floor, New York, NY 10006, USA

477 Williamstown Road, Port Melbourne, VIC 3207, Australia

314–321, 3rd Floor, Plot 3, Splendor Forum, Jasola District Centre, New Delhi – 110025, India

103 Penang Road, #05-06/07, Visioncrest Commercial, Singapore 238467

Torre de los Parques, Colonia Tlacoquemécatl del Valle, Mexico City CP 03200, Mexico

Cambridge University Press & Assessment is a department of the University of Cambridge.

We share the University's mission to contribute to society through the pursuit of education, learning and research at the highest international levels of excellence.

www.cambridge.org
Information on this title: www.cambridge.org/9781316622476

First published 1990
Second edition 1997
Third edition 2005
Fourth edition 2013
Fifth edition 2017
Fifth edition update published 2021

40 39 38 37 36 35 34 33 32 31 30 29

Printed in Poland by Opolgraf

A catalogue record for this publication is available from the British Library.

ISBN 978-1-009-04044-0 Student's Book 1 with eBook
ISBN 978-1-009-04047-1 Student's Book 1A with eBook
ISBN 978-1-009-04048-8 Student's Book 1B with eBook
ISBN 978-1-009-04063-1 Student's Book 1 with Digital Pack
ISBN 978-1-009-04064-8 Student's Book 1A with Digital Pack
ISBN 978-1-009-04065-5 Student's Book 1B with Digital Pack
ISBN 978-1-316-62247-6 Workbook 1
ISBN 978-1-316-62254-4 Workbook 1A
ISBN 978-1-316-62266-7 Workbook 1B
ISBN 978-1-108-40606-2 Teacher's Edition 1
ISBN 978-1-316-62226-1 Class Audio 1
ISBN 978-1-009-04066-2 Full Contact 1 with Digital Pack
ISBN 978-1-009-04067-9 Full Contact 1A with Digital Pack
ISBN 978-1-009-04068-6 Full Contact 1B with Digital Pack
ISBN 978-1-108-40306-1 Presentation Plus 1

Additional resources for this publication at cambridgeone.org

Contents

Credits

The authors and publishers acknowledge the following sources of copyright material and are grateful for the permissions granted. While every effort has been made, it has not always been possible to identify the sources of all the material used, or to trace all copyright holders. If any omissions are brought to our notice, we will be happy to include the appropriate acknowledgements on reprinting and in the next update to the digital edition, as applicable.

Key: TL = Top Left, BL = Below Left, TR = Top Right, BR = Below Right, T = Top, BC = Below Centre, B = Below, R = Right, L = Left, TC = Top Centre, C = Centre.

Illustrations

Pablo Gallego (Beehive Illustration): 42, 53, 65, 78, 91; **Thomas Girard** (Good Illustration): 3, 25, 50, 72, 92; **Quino Marin** (The Organisation): 2, 47, 54, 66; **Gavin Reece** (New Division): 15, 48, 52(B); **Paul Williams** (Sylvie Poggio Artists): 51.

Photos

Back cover (woman with whiteboard): Jenny Acheson/Stockbyte/GettyImages; Back cover (whiteboard): Nemida/GettyImages; Back cover (man using phone): Betsie Van Der Meer/Taxi/GettyImages; Back cover (woman smiling): PeopleImages.com/DigitalVision/GettyImages; Back cover (name tag): Tetra Images/GettyImages; Back cover (handshake): David Lees/Taxi/GettyImages; p. 1: Jon Feingersh/Blend Images/Brand X Pictures/GettyImages; p. 4 (TL): Juanmonino/iStock/GettyImages Plus/GettyImages; p. 4 (BL): Caiaimage/Chris Ryan/OJO+/GettyImages; p. 4 (TR): XiXinXing/GettyImages; p. 4 (BR): powerofforever/E+/GettyImages; p. 5: PeopleImages/DigitalVision/GettyImages; p. 6: Martin Barraud/Caiaimage/GettyImages; p. 7 (photo 1): Jetta Productions/Blend Images/GettyImages; p. 7 (photo 2): Oleksandr Rupeta/NurPhoto/GettyImages; p. 7 (photo 3): Hill Street Studios/Blend Images/GettyImages; p. 7 (photo 4): Jupiterimages/Photolibrary/GettyImages; p. 8: Monty Rakusen/Cultura/GettyImages; p. 9: Matt Hage/Design Pics/First Light/GettyImages; p. 10 (TL): Digital Vision/DigitalVision/GettyImages; p. 10 (TR): Hybrid Images/Cultura/GettyImages; p. 10 (BR): kali9/E+/GettyImages; p. 11: kali9/E+/GettyImages; p. 12 (T): Hybrid Images/Cultura/GettyImages; p. 12 (BL): Visage/Stockbyte/GettyImages; p. 12 (BC): segawa7/iStock/GettyImages Plus/GettyImages; p. 12 (BR): asterix0597/E+/GettyImages; p. 13: Westend61/GettyImages; p. 14: Robert Niedring/Alloy/GettyImages; p. 16 (silver earrings): JohnGollop/iStock/GettyImages Plus/GettyImages; p. 16 (gold earrings): cobalt/iStock/GettyImages Plus/GettyImages; p. 16 (leather coat): bonetta/iStock/GettyImages Plus/GettyImages; p. 16 (wool coat): DonNichols/E+/GettyImages; p. 16 (orange shirt): rolleiflextlr/iStock/GettyImages Plus/GettyImages; p. 16 (gray shirt): popovaphoto/iStock/GettyImages Plus/GettyImages; p. 16 (cotton dresses): Evgenii Karamyshev/Hemera/GettyImages Plus/GettyImages; p. 16 (silk dresses): Paolo_Toffanin/iStock/GettyImages Plus/GettyImages; p. 17 (gold ring): Image Source/GettyImages; p. 17 (silver ring): ProArtWork/E+/GettyImages; p. 17 (tablet): luismmolina/E+/GettyImages; p. 17 (laptop computer): Howard Kingsnorth/The Image Bank/GettyImages; p. 17 (hiking boots): AlexRaths/iStock/GettyImages Plus/GettyImages; p. 17 (sneakers): badmanproduction/iStock/GettyImages Plus/GettyImages; p. 17 (wool gloves): popovaphoto/iStock/GettyImages Plus/GettyImages; p. 17 (leather gloves): Hugh Threlfall/Stockbyte/GettyImages; p. 17 (black sunglasses): Vladimir Liverts/Hemera/GettyImages Plus/GettyImages; p. 17 (white sunglasses): Dimedrol68/iStock/GettyImages Plus/GettyImages; p. 18 (photo 3): csfotoimages/iStock/GettyImages Plus/GettyImages; p. 18 (photo 1): Donald Iain Smith/Moment/GettyImages; p. 18 (photo 4): goir/iStock/GettyImages Plus/GettyImages; p. 18 (photo 2): Marc Romanelli/Blend Images/GettyImages; p. 19 (T): Larry Busacca/GettyImages Entertainment/GettyImages North America/GettyImages; p. 19 (B): Steve Granitz/WireImage/GettyImages; p. 20 (photo 1): Brian Bahr/GettyImages North America/GettyImages; p. 20 (photo 2): Phillip Faraone/GettyImages North America/GettyImages; p. 20 (photo 3): Anthony Harvey/GettyImages Entertainment/GettyImages Europe/GettyImages; p. 20 (photo 4): Taylor Hill/FilmMagic/GettyImages; p. 20 (BR): Jon Kopaloff/FilmMagic/GettyImages; p. 21 (R): DianaHirsch/E+/GettyImages; p. 21 (L): ILM/Universal Studios/GettyImages; p. 23 (T): Shirlaine Forrest/WireImage/GettyImages; p. 23 (B): Moof/Cultura/GettyImages; p. 24 (T): Mike Windle/GettyImages Entertainment/GettyImagesNorth America/GettyImages; p. 24 (B): Donald Miralle/DigitalVision/GettyImages; p. 26: Copyright Anek/Moment/GettyImages; p. 27 (photo 1): Echo/Cultura/GettyImages; p. 27 (photo 2): Juice Images/Cultura/GettyImages; p. 27 (photo 3): Christopher Hope-Fitch/Moment/GettyImages; p. 27 (photo 4): sjenner13/iStock/GettyImages Plus/GettyImages; p. 27 (photo 5): Hero Images/GettyImages; p. 30 (L): Soumen Nath Photography/Moment Open/GettyImages; p. 30 (R): Chaos/The Image Bank/GettyImages; p. 31 (L): Tetra Images/GettyImages; p. 31 (R): John Freeman/Dorling Kindersley/GettyImages; p. 33 (T): Westend61/GettyImages; p. 33 (B): Adam Gault/Photodisc/GettyImages; p. 34 (T): Camilla Watson/AWL Images/GettyImages; p. 34 (C): Stephen McCarthy/Sportsfile/GettyImages; p. 34 (B): PhotoAlto/Laurence Mouton/PhotoAlto Agency RF Collections/GettyImages; p. 35: Koji Aoki/Aflo/GettyImages; p. 36: PeopleImages/DigitalVision/GettyImages; p. 37: Jan Speiser/EyeEm/GettyImages; p. 38 (L): PeopleImages/DigitalVision/GettyImages; p. 38 (R): asiseeit/E+/GettyImages; p. 40 (T): PRASIT CHANSAREEKORN/Moment/GettyImages; p. 40 (B): Tuul and Bruno Morandi/Photolibrary/GettyImages; p. 41 (T): Boy_Anupong/Moment/GettyImages; p. 41 (B): John W Banagan/Lonely Planet Images/GettyImages; p. 46 (L): Allison Michael Orenstein/The Image Bank/GettyImages; p. 46 (R): Plume Creative/DigitalVision/GettyImages; p. 49: Jim Franco/Taxi/GettyImages; p. 52 (boots): StockPhotosArt/iStock/GettyImages Plus/GettyImages; p. 52 (cap): ljpat/E+/GettyImages; p. 52 (dress): pidjoe/E+/GettyImages; p. 52 (high heels): LOVE_LIFE/iStock/GettyImages Plus/GettyImages; p. 52 (jeans): gofotograf/iStock/GettyImages Plus/GettyImages; p. 52 (jewelry): DEA/L. DOUGLAS/De Agostini Editorial/GettyImages; p. 52 (necktie): WilshireImages/E+/GettyImages; p. 52 (shirt): Alex Cao/Photodisc/GettyImages; p. 52 (shorts): stocksnapper/iStock/GettyImages Plus/GettyImages; p. 52 (sneakers): Tevarak/iStock/GettyImages Plus/GettyImages; p. 52 (suit): bonetta/iStock/GettyImages Plus/GettyImages; p. 52 (T-shirt): GaryAlvis/E+/GettyImages; p. 55 (T): Blake Little/Stone/GettyImages; p. 55 (C): Jenner Images/Moment Open/GettyImages; p. 55 (B): Kevin Kozicki/Image Source/GettyImages; p. 56: Barry Austin Photography/Iconica/GettyImages; p. 57 (photo 1): sutichak/iStock/GettyImages Plus/GettyImages; p. 57 (photo 2): Koichi Kamoshida/Photolibrary/GettyImages; p. 57 (photo 3): Westend61/GettyImages; p. 57 (photo 4): Paul Bradbury/OJO Images/GettyImages; p. 57 (photo 5): Jan Hetfleisch/GettyImages Europe/GettyImages; p. 57 (photo 6): Halfdark/GettyImages; p. 58 (T): Jupiterimages/Photos.com/GettyImages Plus/GettyImages; p. 58 (B): Nmaverick/iStock/GettyImages Plus/GettyImages; p. 59 (text messaging): skynesher/E+/GettyImages; p. 59 (rugby match): Stewart Cohen/Photolibrary/GettyImages; p. 59 (sushi): Steve Brown Photography/Photolibrary/GettyImages; p. 59 (houston): Gavin Hellier/Photographer's Choice/GettyImages; p. 60: Sam Edwards/Caiaimage/GettyImages; p. 61 (L): Martin Puddy/Stone/GettyImages; p. 61 (R): Karina Wang/Photographer's Choice/GettyImages; p. 62 (L): jimkruger/iStock/GettyImages Plus/GettyImages; p. 62 (C): AzmanL/iStock/GettyImages Plus/GettyImages; p. 62 (R): Jonas Gratzer/LightRocket/GettyImages; p. 63 (T): Alberto Manuel Urosa Toledano/Moment/GettyImages; p. 63 (B): DUCEPT Pascal/hemis.fr/GettyImages; p. 64 (BL): Sungjin Kim/Moment Open/GettyImages; p. 64 (TC): RODRIGO BUENDIA/AFP/GettyImages; p. 64 (BR): Andrea Pistolesi/Photolibrary/GettyImages; p. 65: JTB/UIG/GettyImages; p. 68: BSIP/UIG/GettyImages; p. 69: KidStock/Blend Images/GettyImages; p. 70: YinYang/E+/GettyImages; p. 71: Ariel Skelley/Blend Images/GettyImages; p. 73 (photo 1): Peter Dazeley/Photographer's Choice/GettyImages; p. 73 (photo 2): whitewish/E+/GettyImages; p. 73 (photo 3): Chuck Kahn/EyeEm/GettyImages; p. 73 (photo 4): lisafx/iStock/GettyImages Plus/GettyImages; p. 73 (photo 5): TUGIO MURATA/amanaimagesRF/GettyImages; p. 73 (photo 6): Creative Crop/DigitalVision/GettyImages; p. 74 (greasy): David Crunelle/EyeEm/GettyImages; p. 74 (bland): Howard Shooter/GettyImages; p. 74 (rich): Johner Images/GettyImages; p. 74 (salty): Creativ Studio Heinemann/GettyImages; p. 74 (healthy): Verdina Anna/Moment/GettyImages; p. 75 (Carlota): andresr/E+/GettyImages; p. 75 (Luka): NicolasMcComber/E+/GettyImages; p. 75 (Adam): David Harrigan/Canopy/GettyImages; p. 76 (broccoli): Kevin Summers/Photographer's Choice/GettyImages; p. 76 (sushi): Food Image Source/StockFood Creative/GettyImages; p. 76 (cream cone): dlerick/E+/GettyImages; p. 77: gchutka/E+/GettyImages; p. 79 (T): Richard Roscoe/Stocktrek Images/GettyImages; p. 79 (C): www.sierralara.com/Moment/GettyImages; p. 79 (B): Yevgen Timashov/Cultura/GettyImages; p. 80: Ulf Andersen/GettyImages Europe/GettyImages; p. 81 (Badwater Basin): David ToussaintMoment/GettyImages; p. 81 (Suez Canal): Jacques Marais/Gallo Images/GettyImages; p. 81 (Mount Waialeale): M Swiet Productions/Moment Open/GettyImages; p. 82: Christian Vorhofer/imageBROKER/GettyImages; p. 83 (Angel Falls): Jane Sweeney/AWL Images/GettyImages; p. 83 (Yangtze River): View Stock/GettyImages; p. 83 (Antarctica): Michael Nolan/robertharding/GettyImages; p. 83 (Rain forest): JohnnyLye/iStock/GettyImages Plus/GettyImages; p. 83 (Grand Canyon): Stephanie Hohmann/EyeEm/GettyImages; p. 84: GlobalP/iStock/GettyImages Plus/GettyImages; p. 86: Emilio Cobos/Euroleague Basketball/GettyImages; p. 87 (go to park): Feverpitched/iStock/GettyImages Plus/GettyImages; p. 87 (go to concerts): Yuri_Arcurs/DigitalVision/GettyImages; p. 87 (have parties): SolStock/E+/GettyImages; p. 87 (see plays): VisitBritain/Eric Nathan/Britain On View/GettyImages; p. 87 (watch horror movies): Crazytang/E+/GettyImages; p. 87 (go on picnics): Kentaroo Tryman/Maskot/GettyImages; p. 88 (Hannah): Dianne Avery Photography/GettyImages; p. 88 (Pablo): Jacqueline Veissid/Blend Images/GettyImages; p. 88 (Richard): Laura Doss/Image Source/GettyImages; p. 88 (Lien): iPandastudio/iStock/GettyImages Plus/GettyImages; p. 88 (Kalil): Juanmonino/E+/GettyImages; p. 88 (Rachel): Westend61/GettyImages; p. 88 (Eliana): billnoll/E+/GettyImages; p. 88 (Daichi): petekarici/iStock/GettyImages Plus/GettyImages; p. 90: ichaka/E+/GettyImages; p. 93 (L): Paul Bradbury/Caiaimage/GettyImages; p. 93 (TR): Hero Images/GettyImages; p. 93 (CR): Hero Images/DigitalVision/GettyImages; p. 94: Zero Creatives/Cultura/GettyImages; p. 95 (T): DragonImages/iStock/GettyImages Plus/GettyImages; p. 95 (C): agentry/iStock/GettyImages Plus/GettyImages; p. 95 (B): Digital Vision/Photodisc/GettyImages; p. 96: Deb Snelson/Moment/GettyImages.

1 Where are you from?

1 Write about yourself.

My first name is ______________________.

My last name is ______________________.

Please call me ______________________.

I'm from ______________________.

2 Put the words in order to make questions. Then answer the questions.

1. class your how English is

   A: How is your English class?

   B: It's pretty interesting.

2. name teacher's your what's

   A: ______________________?

   B: ______________________.

3. from your teacher where is

   A: ______________________?

   B: ______________________.

4. your what friends' are names

   A: ______________________?

   B: ______________________.

5. classmates what your are like

   A: ______________________?

   B: ______________________.

3 Choose the correct responses.

1. **A:** Hi, I'm Diane.
   B: *Oh, hi. I'm Peter.*
   - Oh, hi. I'm Peter.
   - What do people call you?
2. **A:** My name is Bill Matory.
   B: ________________
   - Nice to meet you, Bill.
   - Let's go and say hello.
3. **A:** Hello. I'm a new student here.
   B: ________________
   - Thanks.
   - Welcome.
4. **A:** I'm sorry. What's your name again?
   B: ________________
   - P-A-R-K.
   - Eun-ha Park.
5. **A:** How do you spell your first name?
   B: ________________
   - I'm Akira.
   - A-K-I-R-A.
6. **A:** What do people call you?
   B: ________________
   - It's Angela Young.
   - Everyone calls me Angie.

4 Look at the answers. What are the questions?

1. **Agent:** What *'s your name?*
   Silvia: My name's Silvia.
2. **Agent:** What ________________
   Silvia: My last name's Garcia.
3. **Agent:** Who ________________
   Silvia: That's my husband.
4. **Agent:** What ________________
   Silvia: His name is Gustavo.
5. **Agent:** Where ________________
   Silvia: We're from Venezuela.
6. **Agent:** Who ________________
   Silvia: They're my children.

5 Choose the correct words.

1. That's Antonio. ___He___ is in my class. (He / His)
2. I'm from Barcelona, Spain. ________ is a beautiful city. (It / It's)
3. Excuse me. What's ________ last name again? (you / your)
4. They're my classmates. ________ names are Jill and Tae-min. (They / Their)
5. ________ name is Naoko. Please call me Nao. (I / My)
6. This is Ellen's husband. ________ name is Tim. (His / Her)
7. My parents are on vacation. ________ are in Australia. (We / They)
8. We have English at 10:00. ________ classroom number is 108-C. (Our / We)

6 Complete this conversation with *am, are,* or *is.*

Amber: Who ___are___ the men over there, Ethan?

Ethan: Oh, they ________ on my baseball team. Let me introduce you. Hi, Pablo, this ________ Amber Fox.

Pablo: Nice to meet you, Amber.

Amber: Nice to meet you, too. Where ________ you from?

Pablo: I ________ from Cuba.

Ethan: And this ________ Marco. He ________ from Brazil.

Lisa: Hi, Marco.

7 Hello and welcome!

A Read these four student biographies. Then complete the chart below.

INTERNATIONAL LANGUAGE SCHOOL

Every month, we meet new students at the school. This month, we want to introduce four new students to you. Please say "hello" to them!

Rafael is in English 101. He is from Puebla, Mexico. His first language is Spanish, and he also speaks a little French. He wants to be on the school volleyball team. He says he doesn't play very well, but he wants to learn!

Su-yin is in English 102. She is from Wuhan, China. She says she writes and reads English pretty well, but she needs a lot of practice speaking English. Her first language is Chinese. She wants to play volleyball on the school team.

Fatima is in English 103. She is from Tunis, Tunisia. She speaks Arabic and French. She is an engineering student. She wants to be an engineer. She says she doesn't play any sports. She wants to make a lot of new friends in her class.

Finally, meet **Arun**. He is in Fatima's class. He says he speaks English well, but his writing isn't very good! Arun is from Chennai, India, and his first language is Hindi. He is a soccer player, and he wants to be on the school soccer team.

Name	Where from	Languages	Sports
1. Rafael			
2.	Tunis, Tunisia		
3.		English and Chinese	
4.			soccer

B Write a short biography of a classmate.

____

____

____

____

____

8 Choose the correct sentences to complete this conversation.

- [ ] You, too. Talk to you later.
- [x] Hi, Stacey. I'm Omar. How are you?
- [ ] I really like biology.
- [ ] Yes, I am. I'm an exchange student from Egypt.
- [ ] Yes, he is. We're in Biology 300. Is he your friend?

Stacey: Hello, I'm Stacey.

Omar: Hi, Stacey. I'm Omar. How are you?

Stacey: Pretty good, thanks. Are you a student here?

Omar: ______________________

Stacey: Welcome. Do you like it here? What's your favorite subject?

Omar: ______________________

Stacey: Oh, really? Is Ben Jones in your class?

Omar: ______________________

Stacey: No, he's my brother! Actually, I have to go meet him now. Nice to meet you, Omar.

Omar: ______________________

9 Complete this conversation. Use contractions where possible.

Grammar note: Contractions

Do not use contractions for short answers with *Yes*.

Are you from Argentina?	Is he from Greece?
Yes, I am. (*not* Yes, I'm.)	Yes, he is. (*not* Yes, he's.)

Alex: Hello. ___I'm___ Alex Robles. And this is my sister Celia.

Paola: Hi. ________ Paola Vieira.

Celia: Are you from South America, Paola?

Paola: Yes, ________. ________ from Brazil. Where are you both from?

Alex: ________ from Puerto Rico.

Paola: Are you from San Juan?

Celia: No, ________. ________ from Ponce. By the way, are you in English 101?

Paola: No, ________. I'm in English 102.

10 Look at the answers. What are the questions?

1. **A:** Who's Allison?
   B: Allison is my best friend.
2. **A:** ______________________________
   B: My favorite school subject is history.
3. **A:** ______________________________
   B: No, we're not from Germany. We're from Switzerland.
4. **A:** ______________________________
   B: Yes, it's an interesting class.
5. **A:** ______________________________
   B: Yes, Mary and Yuka are in my class.
6. **A:** ______________________________
   B: Ryan is funny and friendly.
7. **A:** ______________________________
   B: No, Ms. Rogers isn't my English teacher. She's my math teacher.

11 Read the expressions. Which ones say "hello" and which ones say "good-bye"?

	Hello	Good-bye
1. How are you?	☑	☐
2. See you tomorrow.	☐	☐
3. Good night.	☐	☐
4. Good morning.	☐	☐
5. Talk to you later.	☐	☐
6. How's it going?	☐	☐
7. Have a good day.	☐	☐
8. What's up?	☐	☐

12 Answer these questions about yourself. Use contractions where possible.

1. Are you on vacation? ______________________
2. Is your teacher from Canada? ______________________
3. Is your first name popular? ______________________
4. Is your English class in the morning? ______________________
5. Are you from Asia? ______________________
6. Are you a student at a university? ______________________

2 What do you do?

1 Match the correct words to make sentences.

1. A cashier d
2. A vendor ____
3. A babysitter ____
4. A doctor ____
5. A tutor ____
6. A pet sitter ____

a. helps sick people.
b. takes care of animals.
c. sells things.
d. takes money and gives change.
e. takes care of children.
f. helps students with their school work.

2 Write sentences using *He* or *She*.

1. I'm a mechanic. I fix cars. I work in a garage.

He's a mechanic. He fixes cars.

He works in a garage.

2. I'm a cook. I cook food. I work in a restaurant.

She ____________________

____

3. I'm a math teacher. I teach math to students. I work in a school.

She ____________________

____

4. I'm a taxi driver. I drive a car. I take people to places they want to go.

He ____________________

____

3 Write *a* or *an* in the correct places.

Grammar note: Articles *a* and *an*

Use *a* + singular noun before a consonant sound.

Use *an* + singular noun before a vowel sound.

He is **a c**arpenter. He is **an a**ccountant.

He is **a g**ood carpenter. He is **an e**xpensive accountant.

Do not use *a* or *an* + plural nouns.

They are good carpenter**s**. They are expensive accountant**s**.

1. He's *a* carpenter. He works for *a* construction company. He builds schools and houses.
2. She's office manager. She works for large company. It's interesting job.
3. He works in restaurant. He's server. He's also part-time student. He takes business class in the evening.
4. She works for travel company. She arranges tours. She's travel agent.
5. He has difficult job. He's flight attendant. He works on airplane.

4 Choose someone in your family. Write about his or her job.

5 Complete this conversation with the correct words.

Tiffany: What ___does___ (do / does) your brother ________ (do / does), exactly?

Kate: He ________ (work / works) for the city. He's a firefighter.

Tiffany: How ________ (do / does) he ________ (like / likes) it?

Kate: It's an interesting job. He ________ (like / likes) it very much.

But he ________ (work / works) long hours. And what ________ (do / does) you ________ (do / does)?

Tiffany: I'm a student. I ________ (study / studies) geography.

Kate: Oh, really? Where ________ (do / does) you ________ (go / goes) to school?

Tiffany: I ________ (go / goes) to Matthews University. My brother ________ (go / goes) there, too.

Kate: Really? And what ________ (do / does) he ________ (study / studies)?

Tiffany: He ________ (study / studies) graphic design.

Kate: That sounds interesting.

6 Complete the questions in this conversation.

Tom: ___Where do you work?___

Ray: I work for Brady Corporation.

Tom: And what ________________ there?

Ray: I'm an accountant.

Tom: An accountant? How ________________

Ray: I like numbers, so it's a great job. And what ________________

Tom: I'm a teacher.

Ray: Really? What ________________

Tom: I teach accounting!

7 Interesting jobs

Read these two interviews. Answer the questions.

Today, Job Talk interviews two people with interesting jobs.

Job Talk: Oliver, where do you work?

Oliver: Well, I guess I work in the sky.

Job Talk: In the sky? What do you do?

Oliver: I'm a flight attendant. I work on the international flight from Miami to Recife, Brazil.

Job Talk: That's really interesting. What do you like best about your job?

Oliver: I really like to travel and to meet people. So my job is perfect for me.

Job Talk: Do you speak Portuguese?

Oliver: I speak a little. I carry my dictionary everywhere I go!

Job Talk: What do you do, Lucy?

Lucy: I'm a security guard at Matthews University.

Job Talk: That sounds difficult. What is the hardest thing about your job?

Lucy: Well, people break the rules at the university, and I have to stop them.

Job Talk: Are people unfriendly to you?

Lucy: Sometimes, but most of the students are very nice.

Job Talk: And what do you like best about your job?

Lucy: Well, some days the university is quiet. I get to read a lot of books!

1. What does Oliver do? He ____________________
2. Where does he work? ____________________
3. How does Oliver learn Portuguese? ____________________
4. What does Lucy do? She ____________________
5. Where does she work? ____________________
6. What is the hardest part of her job? ____________________

8 Meet Patricio. Write questions about him using *What, Where, When,* and *How.*

1. What does he do?
2. ____________________
3. ____________________
4. ____________________

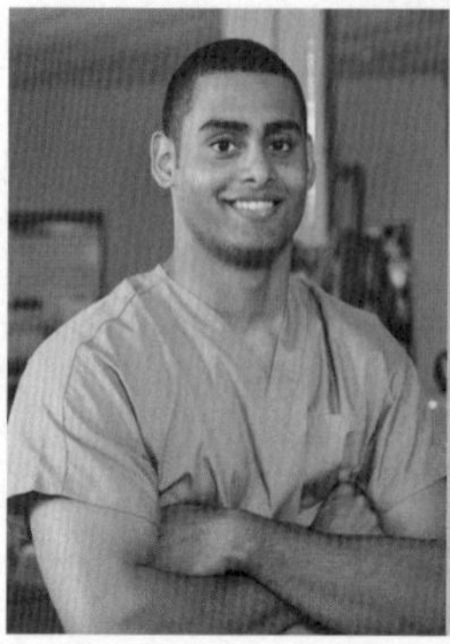

Mercy Hospital

Patricio Cardozo
Registered Nurse,
Night Shift

9 How does Patricio spend his weekends? Complete this paragraph with the words from the box.

☐ around	☐ at	☐ before	☐ early
☐ in	☐ late	☑ on	☐ until

Everyone knows Patricio at the hospital. Patricio is a part-time nurse. He works at night on weekends. ____On____ Saturdays and Sundays, Patricio sleeps most of the day and wakes up a little ____________ nine ____________ the evening, usually at 8:45 or 8:50. He has breakfast very late, ____________ 9:30 or 10:00 P.M.! He watches television ____________ eleven o'clock and then starts work ____________ midnight. ____________ in the morning, usually around 5:00 A.M., he leaves work, has a little snack, goes home, goes to bed, and sleeps ____________. It's a perfect schedule for Patricio. He's a pre-med student on weekdays at a local college.

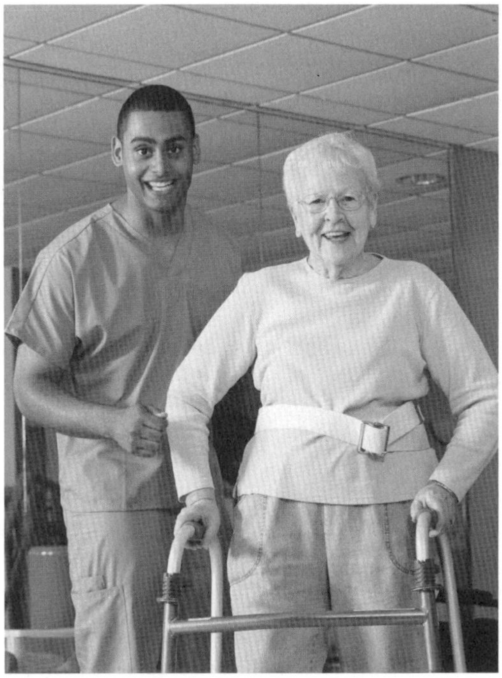

10 Choose the correct words to complete the sentences.

1. Avery is a tour guide. She ____takes____ (answers / takes / writes) people on tours.
2. Stella ____________ (does / goes / starts) to bed after midnight.
3. Bonnie ____________ (answers / gets / starts) up early in the morning.
4. What ____________ (does / goes / serves) your sister do?
5. Roland ____________ (answers / serves / starts) work at 8:00 A.M.
6. My brother works in a bookstore. He ____________ (answers / sells / works) books and magazines.
7. The Havana Garden restaurant ____________ (serves / takes / writes) good Cuban food.
8. Dan ____________ (serves / does / works) his school work on his new computer.
9. Nunu ____________ (goes / sells / writes) about 30 emails a day.
10. David is a receptionist. He ____________ (answers / starts / types) the phone and greets people.
11. Miguel ____________ (does / takes / works) in a restaurant.

11 Choose the sentences in the box that have the same meaning as the sentences below.

- [ ] He goes to the university.
- [ ] She cares for people's pets.
- [ ] She stays up late.
- [ ] What does he do?
- [x] She's a fitness instructor.
- [ ] He works part-time.

1. She teaches exercise classes.
   She's a fitness instructor.
2. What's his job?
   ____
3. She's a pet sitter.
   ____
4. He's a student.
   ____
5. She goes to bed at midnight.
   ____
6. He works three hours every day.
   ____

12 Fill in the missing words or phrases from these job advertisements.

1.
- [ ] at night
- [ ] part-time
- [x] servers
- [ ] weekends

2.
- [ ] interesting
- [ ] Japanese
- [ ] tours
- [ ] student

3.
- [ ] at
- [ ] in
- [ ] manager
- [ ] weekends

Help Wanted

Larry's Diner needs *servers*. Work during the day or ______________, weekdays or ______________, full-time or ______________.
Call 901–555–1977.

______________ job for a language ______________. Take people on ______________. Evenings only. Need good English and ______________ skills.
Email Brenda at Brenda44@cup.org.

We need a great office ______________! Work Monday through Friday, no ______________. Start work ______________ 9:00 ______________ the morning.

3 How much are these?

1 Choose the correct sentences to complete this conversation.

- [ ] Oh, James. Thank you very much.
- [ ] Well, I like it, but it's expensive.
- [ ] Which one?
- [x] Which ones?
- [ ] Yes. But I don't really like yellow.

James: Look at those pants, Linda.
Linda: Which ones?
James: The yellow ones over there. They're nice.
Linda: ______________________
James: Hmm. Well, what about that sweater? It's perfect for you.
Linda: ______________________
James: This blue one.
Linda: ______________________
James: Hey, let me buy it for you. It's a present!
Linda: ______________________

2 Complete these conversations with *How much is/are . . . ?* and *this, that, these,* or *those.*

1. **A:** How much is this blouse right here?
   B: It's $47.95.
2. **A:** ______________________ glasses over there?
   B: They're $87.
3. **A:** ______________________ sneakers right here?
   B: They're $79.99.
4. **A:** ______________________ cat over there?
   B: That's *my* cat, and he's not for sale!

3 Write the plurals of these words.

Spelling note: Plural nouns

Most words		**Words ending in -*ss*, -*sh*, -*ch*, and -*x***	
cap	cap**s**	glass	glass**es**
shoe	shoe**s**	dish	dish**es**
		watch	watch**es**
Words ending in -*f* and -*fe*		**Words ending in consonant + *y***	
shelf	shel**ves**	country	countr**ies**
knife	kni**ves**		

1. ring ___rings___
2. glove ______
3. party ______
4. boy ______
5. tie ______
6. box ______
7. scarf ______
8. blouse ______
9. T-shirt ______
10. hairbrush ______
11. computer ______
12. dress ______

4 What do you think of these prices? Write a response.

That's cheap. That's not bad. That's reasonable. That's pretty expensive!

1. $250 for a wool sweater
   That's pretty expensive!
2. $30 for a silk tie
   ______
3. $180 for a cotton dress
   ______
4. $40 for a gold necklace
   ______
5. $15 for three T-shirts
   ______
6. $80 for a leather belt
   ______

5 Choose the correct words to complete the conversations.

1. **Shirley:** I like ___those___ earrings over there.
(that / those)

Clerk: Which ____________?
(one / ones)

Shirley: The small gold ____________.
(one / ones)

Clerk: ____________ $399.
(It's / They're)

Shirley: Oh, they're expensive!

2. **George:** Excuse me. How much are ____________ pants?
(that / those)

Clerk: ____________ only $65.
(It's / They're)

George: And how much is ____________ shirt?
(this / these)

Clerk: Which ____________?
(one / ones)

They're all different.

George: This green ____________.
(one / ones)

Clerk: ____________ $47.
(It's / They're)

3. **Clerk:** Good afternoon.

Martina: Oh, hi. How much is ____________ watch?
(this / these)

Clerk: ____________ $195.
(It's / They're)

Martina: And how much is that ____________?
(one / ones)

Clerk: ____________ $99.
(It's / They're)

Martina: That's not bad. I'll take it!

6 What do you make from these materials? Complete the chart using words from the box. (You will use words more than once.)

belt	boots	bracelet	button	gloves	hairbrush
jacket	necklace	pants	ring	shirt	

Cotton	Gold	Leather	Plastic	Silk	Wool
gloves					

7 Make comparisons using the words given. Add *than* if necessary.

silver earrings

1. **A:** Hey, look at these silver earrings! They're nice. And they're ___*cheaper than*___ those gold earrings. (cheap)
   B: But they're ______________ the gold ones. (small)
   A: Well, yeah. The gold ones are ______________ the silver ones. (big) But $400 is a lot of money!

gold earrings

leather coat

2. **A:** This leather coat is ______________ the wool one. (attractive)
   B: Yes, but the wool one is ______________. (warm)

wool coat

orange shirt

3. **A:** This orange shirt is an interesting color!
   B: Yes, but the color is ______________ the design. (pretty)
   A: The design isn't bad.
   B: I think the pattern on that gray shirt is ______________ the pattern on this orange one. (good)

gray shirt

cotton dresses

4. **A:** These cotton dresses are nice.
   B: Yes, but the silk ones are ______________. (nice)
   A: They're also ______________. (expensive)

silk dresses

8 Complete the chart. Use the words from the box.

☑ boots	☐ MP3 player	☐ tablet
☐ bracelet	☐ necklace	☐ television
☐ dress	☐ pants	☐ T-shirt
☐ earrings	☐ ring	☐ smartphone

Clothing	Electronics	Jewelry
boots		

9 Answer these questions. Give your own information.

1 gold ring

silver ring

2 tablet

laptop computer

3 hiking boots

sneakers

4 wool gloves

leather gloves

5 black sunglasses

white sunglasses

1. Which ring do you prefer, the silver one or the gold one?
   I prefer the gold one.
2. Which one do you like more, the tablet or the laptop computer?
   ____
3. Which ones do you like more, the hiking boots or the sneakers?
   ____
4. Which ones do you prefer, the wool gloves or the leather gloves?
   ____
5. Which sunglasses do you like better, the black ones or the white ones?
   ____

10 Great gadgets!

A Read these ads. Match the pictures and descriptions.

1. _____ **2.** _____ **3.** _____ **4.** _____

a. Do you want to help the environment and do yard work at the same time? This machine knows when your lawn needs water. It waters your grass, and you don't have to do anything! Save time, save water, and save money! Only $124.99.

b. You can take this with you to the beach or on a picnic. No more uncomfortable towels or blankets! It fills with air in five minutes. Feel like you are sitting in your own living room in the great outdoors! Only $49.50.

c. What's a party without music? Indoors or outdoors, you can have a good time with this small item on a shelf or in a tree. Turn it down to set the mood, or turn it up to start the dancing! Only $299.99.

d. What's it like to swim like a fish? Now is your chance to find out! Put both feet in, get in the water, and feel what it's like to flap instead of kick. If you love to be in the water and dive deep, you need this! $36.

B Check (✓) True or False.

	True	False
1. The garden sensor waters your lawn when it needs more water.	☐	☐
2. The inflatable chair takes about five minutes to fill with air.	☐	☐
3. The Soundbook only works indoors.	☐	☐
4. You need two monofins, one for each foot.	☐	☐

C What's special about a gadget you have? Write a paragraph about it.

____

____

____

____

____

____

____

4 Do you play the guitar?

1 Check (✓) the boxes to complete the survey about music and TV.

A Do you like these types of music?

	I love it!	It's OK.	I don't like it.
pop	☐	☐	☐
classical	☐	☐	☐
hip-hop	☐	☐	☐
rock	☐	☐	☐
jazz	☐	☐	☐

B Do you like these types of TV shows?

	I love them!	They're OK.	I don't like them.
talk shows	☐	☐	☐
reality shows	☐	☐	☐
sitcoms	☐	☐	☐
soap operas	☐	☐	☐
game shows	☐	☐	☐

2 What's your opinion? Answer the questions with the expressions and pronouns in the box.

Yes, I do.	**Object pronouns**
I love . . .	him
I like . . . a lot.	her
No, I don't.	it
I don't like . . . very much.	them
I can't stand . . .	

1. Do you like horror movies?
   Yes, I do. I like them a lot.
2. Do you like Kendrick Lamar?
   ____
3. Do you like heavy metal music?
   ____
4. Do you like mystery books?
   ____
5. Do you like video games?
   ____
6. Do you like Adele?
   ____

Kendrick Lamar

Adele

3 Choose the correct job for each picture.

☐ an actor ☐ an athlete ☐ a pop group ☐ a singer

1. Hope Solo is ____________________

2. Fall Out Boy are ____________________

3. Chris Hemsworth is

____

____

4. Luke Bryan is

____

____

4 Complete these conversations.

1. **Ken:** ___Do___ you ___like___ pop music, Janet?

Janet: Yes, I __________ it a lot. I'm a big fan of Beyoncé.

Ken: Oh, __________ she play the guitar?

Janet: No, she __________, but she's a great dancer.

2. **Alice:** __________ kind of music __________ your parents __________, Jack?

Jack: They __________ country music.

Alice: Who __________ they __________? Jason Aldean?

Jack: No, they __________ like him very much. They prefer Carrie Underwood.

3. **Harold:** Kelly, who's your favorite female singer? __________ you __________ Selena Gomez?

Kelly: No, I __________. I can't stand her. I like Etana.

Harold: I don't know her. What kind of music __________ she sing?

Kelly: She __________ reggae. She's really great!

5 Complete these questions and write answers.

1. What kinds of movies do you like? I like ______
2. ______ is your favorite movie? My favorite ______
3. ______ of movies do you dislike? ______
4. ______ of TV shows do you like? ______
5. ______ is your favorite actor or actress? ______
6. ______ is your favorite song? ______
7. ______ is your favorite rock band? ______
8. ______ is your favorite video game? ______

6 What do you think? Answer the questions.

1. Which are more interesting, action movies or historical dramas?
______
2. Which movies are more exciting, westerns or crime thrillers?
______
3. Which do you like more, musicals or animated movies?
______
4. Which do you prefer, romantic comedies or science fiction movies?
______
5. Which are scarier, horror movies or thrillers?
______

7 Verbs and nouns

A Which nouns often go with these verbs? Complete the chart. Use each noun only once.

listen to	play	watch
music		

- [ ] a basketball game
- [ ] the piano
- [ ] the guitar
- [ ] videos
- [ ] the radio
- [ ] R&B
- [ ] the drums
- [x] music
- [ ] a movie

B Write a sentence using each verb in part A.

1. ______________________________
2. ______________________________
3. ______________________________

8 Movie reviews

A Read the movie reviews. Write the type of movie for each review below the title.

comedy	historical drama	science fiction	crime thriller	horror
travel	documentary	romantic comedy	western	

Movie Reviews

Search

Home News Reviews Listings Box Office Sign in Register

1 Ahead of Time

____

What are high school kids like in the future? This movie gives an answer. It's about a group of school kids in the year 2017. After class one day, they find a time machine behind the school. One of the teens sees a button marked "Year 2500" and presses it. They suddenly travel to the twenty-sixth century! They have many exciting adventures. But do they get back in time for school the next day? Watch and find out.

SCORE ★★★★☆

2 House of Laughs

____

This movie is about a group of six young people in London. They live in the same house in a suburb far from the city center. All of them come from different countries. They speak different languages and have different customs. What happens when they're all under one roof? Watch and laugh! The story is very funny, and the acting is very good. This movie is like a really good TV soap opera, but funnier.

SCORE ★★★★★

3 Coming Up for Air

____

The action never stops in this movie. Police officer Karen Montana wants to catch Mr. X, a notorious gold thief. Mr. X is stealing gold from an old shipwreck at the bottom of the ocean. The only way to catch him is under the water. But Montana's one weakness is that she can't swim and hates the water. Will she catch him? The plot isn't very good, but the surprise ending is worth waiting for. Watch for yourself.

SCORE ★★☆☆☆

B Write down the words in the review that helped you to decide what kind of movie it is.

1. Ahead of Time: future, ______________________________
2. House of Laughs: ______________________________
3. Coming Up for Air: ______________________________

9 Choose the correct responses.

1. **A:** What do you think of "The Voice"?
   B: I'm not a real fan of the show.
   - How about you?
   - I'm not a real fan of the show.
2. **A:** Do you like jazz music?
   B: ______________________
   - I can't stand it.
   - I can't stand them.
3. **A:** There's a soccer game tonight.
   B: ______________________
   - Thanks. I'd love to.
   - Great. Let's go.
4. **A:** Would you like to see a movie this weekend?
   B: ______________________
   - That sounds great!
   - I don't agree.

10 *Yes* or *no*?

A Fabiana is inviting friends to a movie. Do they accept the invitation or not? Check (✓) *Yes* or *No* for each response.

Accept?	Yes	No
1. I'd love to. What time does it start?	☑	☐
2. Thanks, but I don't really like animated movies.	☐	☐
3. That sounds great. Where is it?	☐	☐
4. I'd love to, but I have to work until midnight.	☐	☐
5. Thanks. I'd really like to. When do you want to meet?	☐	☐

B Respond to the invitations.

1. I have tickets to a classical concert on Saturday. Would you like to go?
   ____
2. There's a soccer game tonight. Do you want to go with me?
   ____
3. Meghan Trainor is performing tomorrow at the stadium. Would you like to see her?
   ____

11 Choose the correct phrases to complete these conversations.

1. **Eva:** Do you like pop music, Anita?
(Do you like / Would you like)

Anita: Yes, I do. ______________________ it a lot.
(I like / I'd like)

Eva: There's an Ariana Grande concert on Friday.
______________________ to go with me?
(Do you like / Would you like)

Anita: Yes, ______________________! Thanks.
(I love to / I'd love to)

2. **Marco:** There's a baseball game on TV tonight.
______________________ to come over and watch it?
(Do you like / Would you like)

Tony: ______________________, but I have to study tonight.
(I like to / I'd like to)

Marco: Well, ______________________ basketball?
(do you like / would you like)

Tony: Yes, ______________________. I love it!
(I do / I would)

Marco: There's a game on TV tomorrow at 3:00.
______________________ to watch that with me?
(Do you like / Would you like)

Tony: ______________________. Thanks!
(I like to / I'd love to)

12 Rewrite these sentences. Find another way to say each sentence using the words given.

1. Do you like rap?
What do you think of rap? (think of)
2. Chad doesn't like country music.
____ (can't stand)
3. I think soap operas are great!
____ (love)
4. Celia doesn't like new age music.
____ (be a fan of)
5. Do you want to go to a soccer match?
____ (would like)

5 What an interesting family!

1 Which words are for males? Which are for females? Complete the chart.

☑ aunt	☐ husband	☐ sister
☑ brother	☐ mother	☐ son
☐ daughter	☐ nephew	☐ uncle
☐ father	☐ niece	☐ wife

Males			Females		
brother			aunt		

2 Complete this conversation. Use the present continuous of the verbs given.

Jan: You look tired, Monica. ___Are you studying___ (study) late at night these days?

Monica: No, I'm not. My brother and sister ____________ (stay) with me right now. They keep me up late every night.

Jan: Really, both of them? What ____________ (do) this summer? ____________ (take) classes, too?

Monica: No, they aren't. My brother is on vacation now, but he ____________ (look) for a part-time job here.

Jan: What about your sister? ____________ (work)?

Monica: Yes, she is. She has a part-time job at the university. What about you, Jan? Are you in school this summer?

Jan: Yes, I am. I ____________ (study) two languages.

Monica: Oh, ____________ (take) Korean and Spanish again?

Jan: Well, I'm taking Korean, but now I ____________ (start) Portuguese classes.

Monica: Really? That's exciting!

3 What is another way to say each sentence? Rewrite the sentences using the words in the box.

aunt	mother-in-law	~~uncle~~
granddaughter	son and daughter	wife

1. Anita is Marco's niece.
   Marco is Anita's uncle.
2. John is married to Ann.
   ____
3. My father's sister is a teacher.
   ____
4. We have two children.
   ____
5. My husband's mother is from Mexico.
   ____
6. Willie and Mabel are Brooke's grandparents.
   ____

4 Choose the correct sentences to complete the conversation.

- [ ] Yes, he is. He loves it there.
- [x] No, I'm not. I'm living in Singapore now.
- [ ] Yes, we are. We really love Miami.
- [ ] Yes, I do. I like it a lot.
- [ ] No, they aren't. They're living in Atlanta now.

Singapore

Kathy: Are you still living in Miami, Martin?

Martin: No, I'm not. I'm living in Singapore now.

Kathy: Wow! Do you like it?

Martin: ______________________

Kathy: And is your brother still working in Seoul?

Martin: ______________________

Kathy: And how about your parents? Are they still living in Florida?

Martin: ______________________ How about you and your family, Kathy? Are you still living here?

Kathy: ______________________

5 Complete these sentences. Use the simple present or the present continuous of the verbs given.

1. This is my cousin, Martin.
   He ______lives______ (live) in Houston, but
   he ____________________ (visit) Peru this summer.
   He ____________________ (take) cooking classes there.

2. And these are my parents.
   They ____________________ (work) in Paris this year.
   They ____________________ (be) on vacation right now.

3. Here's a photo of my grandparents.
   They ____________________ (not work) now.
   They ____________________ (be) retired.

4. This is my sister-in-law, Amanda.
   She ____________________ (want) to start her own company.
   She ____________________ (study) business in Australia right now.

5. And this is my nephew, George.
   He ____________________ (go) to high school.
   He ____________________ (like) history, but
   he ____________________ (not like) chemistry.

6 Choose a friend or a family member. Write about him or her using the simple present and present continuous.

____

____

____

____

7 Home or away?

A Answer these questions. Then read the passage.

1. Read the title below. What do you think a "boomerang kid" is?

   ____

2. Are you going to live at home when you leave school? Why or why not?

   ____

BOOMERANG KIDS

Today in the United States, many young adults are returning home to live after they graduate from college. They are being called "boomerang kids," like the Australian hunting stick that comes back after you throw it. Many college graduates can't find the jobs they want right away. Some also have college loans to pay back. They don't have enough money to rent expensive apartments, so they go back home to live with their parents. While they live at home, they are working at jobs with low pay and trying to save money for the future.

Meanwhile, the parents of boomerang kids are feeling the challenges of having their adult children back home. Most understand the problems their kids are having with money and accept that they're living with them again. But their relationships are different now. Some parents expect their kids to keep following their rules and to help around the house. Young adults, on the other hand, want to be independent and to make their own decisions. This creates tension between parents and kids. These boomerangs go out as kids, but they come back as adults.

B Check (✓) True or False. For statements that are false, write the correct information.

Young Adults	True	False
1. "Boomerang kids" are college graduates who don't want to live at home. ______________________	☐	☐
2. Many college graduates are having a difficult time finding a good job. ______________________	☐	☐
3. College graduates who live at home can't save money for the future. ______________________	☐	☐

Parents	True	False
4. Parents are seeing that it can be difficult to have their "boomerang kids" live at home again. ______________________	☐	☐
5. Parents want to do everything for their kids like they did when they were younger. ______________________	☐	☐
6. Parents and kids mostly agree about the rules and expectations of the house. ______________________	☐	☐

8 Arrange the quantifiers from the most to the least.

- [x] all
- [ ] few
- [ ] many
- [ ] most
- [ ] nearly all
- [x] no
- [ ] some

1. all
2. ______
3. ______
4. ______
5. ______
6. ______
7. no

9 Rewrite these sentences about the United States using the quantifiers given.

1. Ninety percent of children go to public schools. Ten percent of children go to private schools.

   Most children go to public schools.

   Few ______

   ______

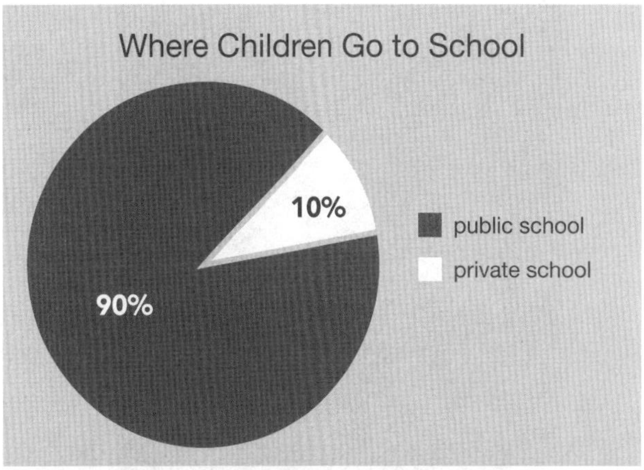

2. Sixty-two percent of young people go to college after they finish high school. Thirty-four percent of young people look for work.

   Many ______

   ______

   Some ______

   ______

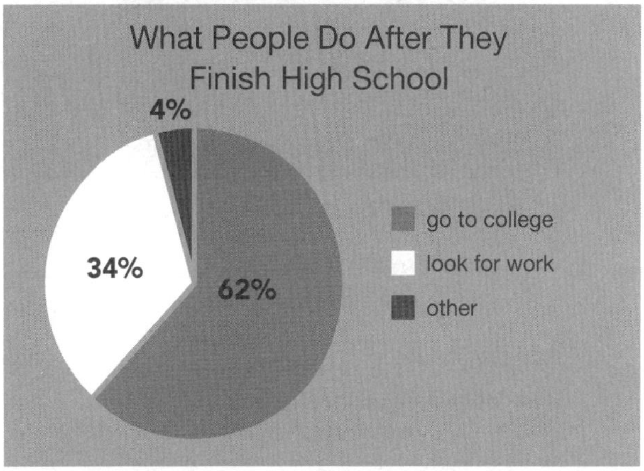

3. Ninety-five percent of people over 65 like to talk to family and friends. Forty-three percent of people over 65 like to spend time on a hobby. Three percent of people over 65 like to play soccer.

   Not many ______

   ______

   A lot of ______

   ______

   Nearly all ______

   ______

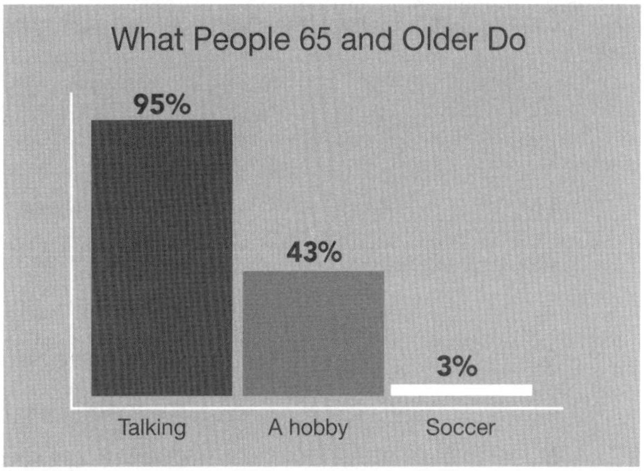

10 Choose the correct words or phrases to complete this paragraph.

In my country, some ___couples___ (couples / cousins / relatives) get married fairly young. Not many marriages ______________ (break up / get divorced / stay together), and nearly all ______________ (divorced / married / single) people remarry. Elderly couples often ______________ (divorce again / move away / live at home) and take care of their grandchildren.

11 Complete these sentences about your country. Use the words in the box.

all	a lot of	few	most	nearly all	no	some

1. ______________ young people go to college.
2. ______________ people study English.
3. ______________ married couples have more than five children.
4. ______________ elderly people have part-time jobs.
5. ______________ students have full-time jobs.
6. ______________ children go to school on Saturdays.

6 How often do you run?

1 Complete the chart. Use words from the box.

baseball	soccer	basketball	volleyball	football
walking	jogging	weight training	Pilates	yoga

Sports	Fitness activities
baseball	

2 Arrange these words to make sentences or questions.

1. often mornings play on we tennis Saturday
   We often play tennis on Saturday mornings.
2. ever Ryan do does yoga
   ______________________________?
3. go do often swimming how you
   ______________________________?
4. go never I almost jogging
   ______________________________.
5. hardly they basketball play ever
   ______________________________.
6. do on you what usually Sundays do
   ______________________________?

3 Use these questions to complete the conversations: *How often do you . . . ? Do you ever . . . ? What do you usually . . . ?*

1. **A:** *Do you ever go bowling?*
   B: Yes, I often go bowling on weekends.
2. **A:** ______________________________
   B: Well, I usually do martial arts or watch TV after work.
3. **A:** ______________________________
   B: Yes, I sometimes play sports on weekends – usually soccer.
4. **A:** ______________________________
   B: I don't exercise very often at all.
5. **A:** ______________________________
   B: No, I never go to the gym on Saturdays.
6. **A:** ______________________________
   B: I usually go jogging four times a week.

4 Keeping fit?

A Check (✓) how often you do each of the things in the chart.

	Every day	Once or twice a week	Sometimes	Not very often	Never
do martial arts	☐	☐	☐	☐	☐
play basketball	☐	☐	☐	☐	☐
exercise	☐	☐	☐	☐	☐
go jogging	☐	☐	☐	☐	☐
go bowling	☐	☐	☐	☐	☐
play soccer	☐	☐	☐	☐	☐
go swimming	☐	☐	☐	☐	☐
do weight training	☐	☐	☐	☐	☐

B Write about your fitness habits using the information in the chart.

____
____
____
____
____
____
____

5 Complete this conversation with the correct prepositions. Write them in the correct places.

Kelly: What time do you go swimming ^in the morning? (around / in / on)

Neil: I always go swimming 7:00. (at / for / on)

How about you, Kelly?

Kelly: I usually go swimming noon. (around / in / with)

I swim about 30 minutes. (at / for / until)

Neil: And do you also play sports your free time? (at / in / until)

Kelly: No, I usually go out my classmates. (around / for / with)

What about you?

Neil: I go to the gym Mondays and Wednesdays. (at / on / until)

And sometimes I go jogging weekends. (for / in / on)

Kelly: Wow! You really like to stay in shape.

6 Complete the sentences. Use the words from the box.

do	ice hockey	soccer	treadmill	goes	jogging
swimming	watches	~~exercises~~	shape	training	

1. Katie never __exercises__. She's a real couch potato.
2. How often do you ____________ martial arts?
3. I like to stay in ____________. I play sports every day.
4. Jeff does weight ____________ every evening. He lifts 50-pound weights.
5. Arturo goes ____________ twice a week. He usually runs about three miles.
6. Miho often ____________ TV in the evening.
7. Maria is on the ____________ team at her high school. She's good at passing the ball.
8. Judy never goes ____________ when the water is cold.
9. Kyle often ____________ bike riding on weekends.
10. I run on the ____________ at the gym three times a week.
11. In Canada, many people like to play ____________ outside in the winter.

7 Sports around the world

A Read the descriptions of three unique sports that are played in different parts of the world. Which sport do you want to try? Why?

Capoeira

Capoeira is a sport that comes from Brazil. It is part martial art, part dance, and part game. The legs do most of the work in this sport. Capoeiristas kick, jump, and dance to the music of stringed instruments, drums, bells, and rattles. Although the two people are fighting and defending themselves, capoeira is really more about movement, speed, and knowing what your opponent is thinking.

Hurling

The game of hurling comes from Ireland. It is the fastest field sport in the world. Hurlers play on a field like soccer but use a stick and a small ball. The stick is used to carry or hit the ball, or players can kick it or slap it with their hands. They try to get the ball over a bar for one point or under the bar into a net for three points. Hurling is a very old sport and similar to modern rugby, soccer, field hockey, and football.

Bashi

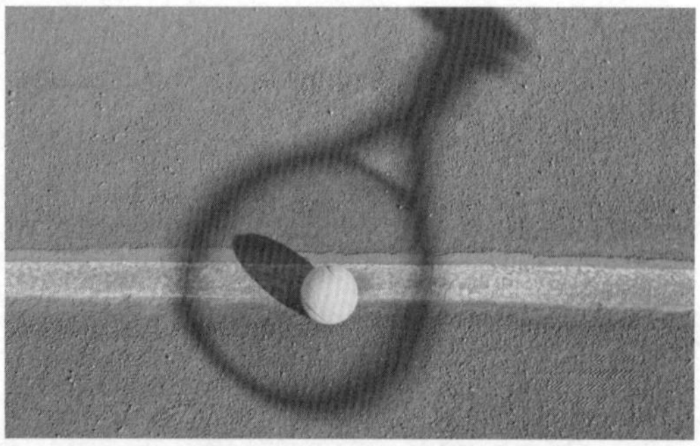

Bashi is a national sport in the Maldives, and only women play it. Between eight and eleven women play on a tennis court with tennis balls and one tennis racket. One player hits a ball with the racket on one side of the net, and players try to catch it on the other side. The woman who hits the ball faces away from the net and has to hit the ball backwards over her head! Women often get injured trying to catch the fast-moving balls with their bare hands.

B What sport do the activities describe? Check (✓) the answers.

	Capoeira	Hurling	Bashi
1. hit a ball backwards	☐	☐	☐
2. run very fast	☐	☐	☐
3. know what your opponent is thinking	☐	☐	☐
4. get a ball in a net	☐	☐	☐
5. move with music	☐	☐	☐
6. hit a ball over a net	☐	☐	☐

8 Choose the correct responses.

1. **A:** How often do you play golf, Monica?
   B: *Once a week.*
   - I guess I'm OK.
   - Once a week.
   - About an hour.
2. **A:** How long do you spend on the golf course?
   B: ____________________
   - About four hours.
   - About average.
   - About three miles.
3. **A:** And how well do you play?
   B: ____________________
   - I'm not very well.
   - I almost never do.
   - I'm about average.
4. **A:** How good are you at other sports?
   B: ____________________
   - Not very good, actually.
   - I sometimes play twice a week.
   - Pretty well, I guess.

9 Look at the answers. Write questions using *how*.

1. **A:** *How long do you spend exercising?*
   B: I don't spend any time at all. In fact, I don't exercise.
2. **A:** ____________________ at playing football?
   B: I'm pretty good at it. I'm on the school team.
3. **A:** ____________________ for a walk?
   B: Almost every day. I really enjoy it.
4. **A:** ____________________
   B: Baseball? Pretty well, I guess. Yeah, I like it a lot.
5. **A:** ____________________
   B: I spend about an hour jogging.

10 Rewrite these sentences. Find another way to say each sentence using the words given.

1. I don't go bike riding very often.
   I hardly ever go bike riding. (hardly ever)
2. Tamara exercises twice a month.
   ______________________ (not very often)
3. Patty tries to keep fit.
   ______________________ (stay in shape)
4. Ricardo often exercises at the gym.
   ______________________ (work out)
5. I go jogging every day after work.
   ______________________ (always)
6. How good are you at tennis?
   ______________________ (play)

11 What do you think about fitness and sports? Answer these questions.

1. Do you like to exercise for a short time or a long time?
   ____
   ____
2. Do you prefer exercising in the morning or in the evening?
   ____
   ____
3. Which do you like better, walking or jogging?
   ____
   ____
4. Which do you like better, team sports or individual sports?
   ____
   ____
5. How good are you at sports like basketball and tennis?
   ____
   ____
6. What is a sport or game you don't like?
   ____
   ____

7 We went dancing!

1 Past tense

A Write the simple past of these regular verbs.

1. watch ___watched___
2. play ____________
3. invite ____________
4. arrive ____________
5. study ____________
6. hurry ____________
7. travel ____________
8. wash ____________
9. look ____________

B Write the simple present form of these irregular simple past verbs.

1. ___eat___ ate
2. ____________ did
3. ____________ met
4. ____________ saw
5. ____________ slept
6. ____________ spent
7. ____________ drove
8. ____________ went

C Use two of the verbs above and write sentences about the past.

Example: ___We saw the Eiffel Tower in Paris last year.___
1. ____
2. ____

2 Use the cues to answer these questions.

1. Where did you go this weekend?
___I went to the zoo.___ (to the zoo)

2. Who did you meet at the party?
____ (a famous artist)

3. What did you buy?
____ (a new pair of jeans)

4. How did you and Mario like the movie?
____ (a lot)

5. Where did Faye and Bob spend their vacation?
____ (in the country)

6. What time did you and Allison get home?
____ (a little after 1:00)

3 What do you like to do alone? With other people? Complete the chart with activities from the box. Then add one more activity to each list.

- cook dinner
- do homework
- exercise
- go shopping
- go to a sports event
- go to the movies
- have a picnic
- play video games
- take a vacation
- watch TV

Activities I like to do alone	Activities I like to do with other people

4 Complete the questions in this conversation.

A: How did you spend the weekend ?

B: I spent the weekend with my sisters.

A: What ______________________?

B: Well, on Saturday, we went shopping.

A: That sounds like fun! What ______________________?

B: I bought a new pair of shoes and a new purse.

A: Where ______________________ on Sunday?

B: We went to an amusement park.

A: Oh, how ______________________?

B: We had a great time. In fact, we stayed there all day.

A: Really? What time ______________________?

B: We got home very late, around midnight.

5 Answer these questions with negative statements. Then add a positive statement using the information in the box.

☐ finish the project on Saturday	☐ take the bus
☐ go out with friends	☐ watch it on TV
☑ stay home all weekend	☐ work all day until six o'clock

1. **A:** Did you and John go to Anne's party on Saturday?
   B: No, we didn't. We stayed home all weekend.
2. **A:** Beth left work at 2:00 yesterday afternoon. Did you go home early, too?
   B: ______
3. **A:** I watched TV all weekend. Did you spend the weekend at home, too?
   B: ______
4. **A:** I saw you and Amy at the library on Saturday. Did you work together on Sunday, too?
   B: ______
5. **A:** Giovanni drove me to work yesterday morning. Did you drive to work?
   B: ______
6. **A:** Sandy went to the baseball game last night. Did you and Martin go to the game?
   B: ______

6 Read about Pamela's week. Match the sentences that have a similar meaning.

A		B
1. She was broke last week.	f	**a.** She had people over.
2. She didn't work on Monday.	____	**b.** She did housework.
3. She worked around the house.	____	**c.** She took the day off.
4. She didn't wash the clothes.	____	**d.** She had a good time.
5. She invited friends for dinner.	____	**e.** She didn't do the laundry.
6. She had a lot of fun.	____	✓ **f.** She spent all her money.

7 Did we take the same trip?

A Read the posts. Who went to Bangkok for the first time?

JOSEPH

We went to Thailand again for our summer vacation. We spent a week in Bangkok and did something every day. We went to the floating market very early one morning. We didn't buy anything there – we just looked. Another day, we went to Wat Phra Kaew, the famous Temple of the Emerald Buddha. Check out my pic!

Then we saw two more temples nearby. We also went on a river trip somewhere outside Bangkok. The best thing about the trip was the food. The next time we have friends over for dinner, I'm going to cook Thai food.

OLIVIA

Last summer, we spent our vacation in Thailand. We were very excited – it was our first trip there. We spent two days in Bangkok. Of course, we got a river taxi to the floating market. We bought some delicious fruit there. I'm posting a picture.

The next day we went to a very interesting temple called the Temple of the Emerald Buddha. We didn't have time to visit any other temples. However, we went to two historic cities – Ayutthaya and Sukhothai. Both have really interesting ruins. Everything was great. It's impossible to say what the best thing was about the trip.

B Who did these things on their trip? Check (✓) all correct answers.

	Joseph	Olivia
1. stayed for two days in Bangkok	☐	☑
2. visited the floating market	☐	☐
3. bought fruit	☐	☐
4. saw some historic ruins	☐	☐
5. traveled on the river	☐	☐
6. loved the food the most	☐	☐
7. enjoyed everything	☐	☐

8 Complete this conversation with *was, wasn't, were,* or *weren't.*

A: How ___was___ your vacation in Thailand, Rich?

B: It ______ great. I really enjoyed it.

A: How long ______ you there?

B: We ______ there for two weeks.

A: ______ you in Bangkok the whole time?

B: No, we ______. We ______ in the mountains for a few days.

A: And how ______ the weather? ______ it good?

B: No, it ______ good at all! In fact, it ______ terrible. The city ______ very hot, and the mountains ______ cold and rainy!

9 Choose the correct questions to complete this conversation.

- [ ] And what was the best part?
- [ ] How long were you in Brazil?
- [x] How was your vacation in South America?
- [ ] And how long were you in Argentina?
- [ ] How was the weather?

A: How was your vacation in South America?

B: It was a great trip. I really enjoyed Brazil and Argentina.

A: ______

B: I was in Brazil for ten days.

A: ______

B: For about eight days.

A: Wow, that's a long time! ______

B: It was hot and sunny the whole time.

A: ______

B: It was definitely the beaches in Brazil. Oh, and we learned the tango in Argentina!

10 Complete the sentences with the correct words or phrases. Use the past tense when necessary.

1. We ____________ a trip to Egypt last summer. (take / make / do)
2. My brothers ____________ at home all weekend. (go dancing / play video games / take a bike ride)
3. I worked really hard in Germany last week. I was there ____________. (in my car / on business / on vacation)
4. I'm sorry I was late. I had to ____________ a phone call. (do / make / go)
5. I stayed home last night and ____________ the laundry. (do / go / make)

11 My kind of vacation

A What do you like to do on vacation? Rank these activities from 1 (you like it the most) to 6 (you like it the least).

____ go to the beach
____ visit historical places
____ go shopping
____ visit museums
____ spend time at home
____ eat good food

B Answer these questions about vacations.

1. How often do you go on vacation?
____
2. How much time do you spend on vacation?
____
3. Who do you usually go with?
____
4. Where do you like to go?
____
5. What do you usually do on vacation?
____

8 How's the neighborhood?

1 Places

A Match the words in columns A and B. Write the names of the places.

A	B	
☑ coffee	☐ campus	**1.** coffee shop
☐ college	☑ shop	**2.**
☐ gas	☐ hotspot	**3.**
☐ grocery	☐ office	**4.**
☐ hair	☐ mall	**5.**
☐ movie	☐ salon	**6.**
☐ post	☐ station	**7.**
☐ shopping	☐ store	**8.**
☐ Wi-Fi	☐ theater	**9.**

B Write questions with *Is there a . . . ?* or *Are there any . . . ?* and the names of places from part A.

1. **A:** I need a haircut. Is there a hair salon near here?
   B: Yes, there's one on Grand Street.
2. **A:** I want to buy some new clothes. ________________ near here?
   B: No, there isn't, but there's one in Center City.
3. **A:** I need to mail this package. ________________ around here?
   B: Yes, there's one next to the bank.
4. **A:** I want to see a movie tonight. ________________ around here?
   B: Yes, there's one in the shopping mall.
5. **A:** We need some gas. ________________ on this street?
   B: No, there aren't, but there are a couple on Second Avenue.
6. **A:** We need to buy some cereal and some apples.
   ________________ near here?
   B: Yes, there's one near the gym on Brown Street.

2 Look at these street maps of Springfield and Riverside. There are ten differences between them. Find the other eight.

Grammar note: *There are; some* and *any*

Positive statement	**Negative statement**
There **are some** Wi-Fi hotspots near the bank.	There **aren't any** Wi-Fi hotspots near the bank.

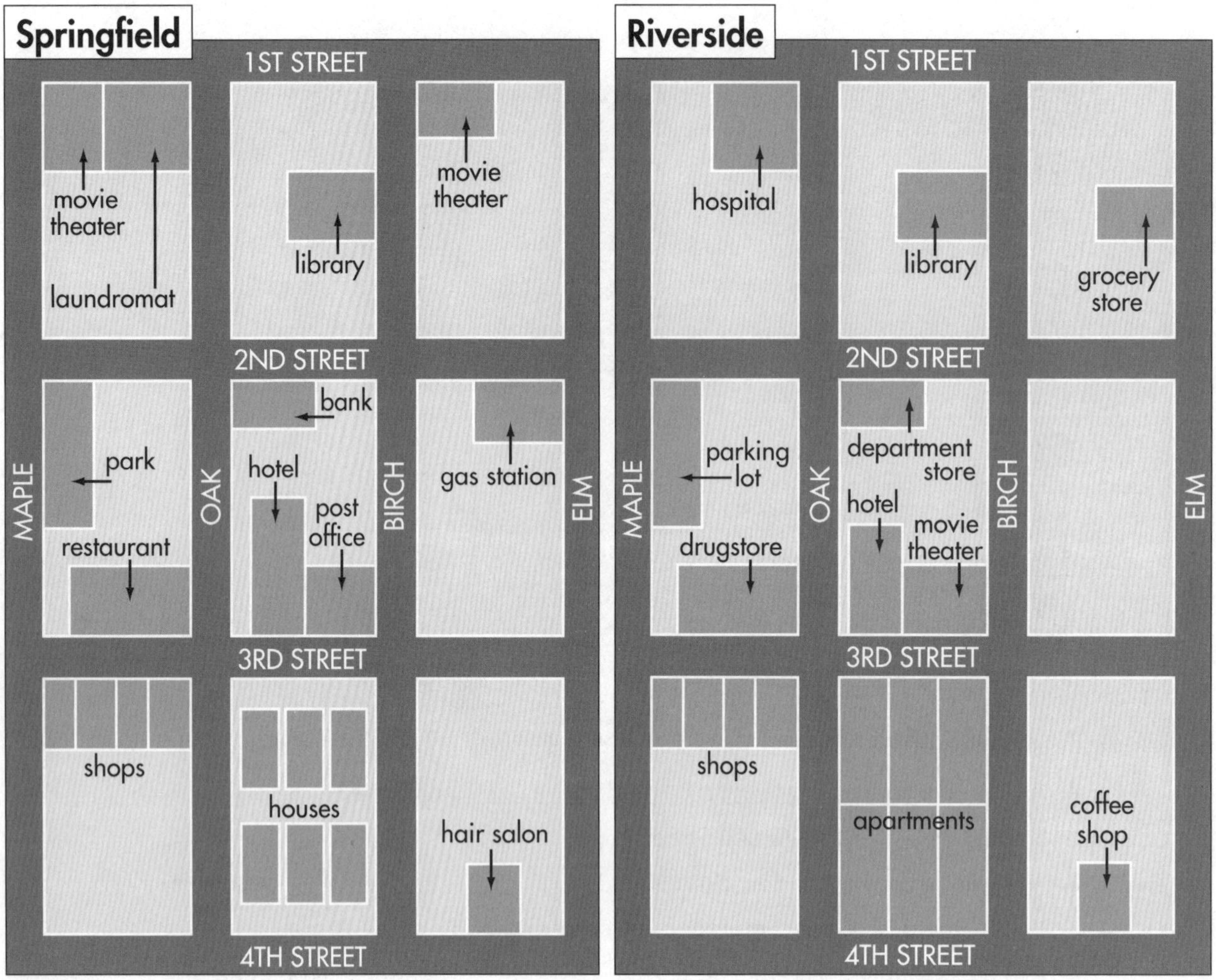

1. There are some movie theaters on 1st Street in Springfield, but there aren't any in Riverside.
2. There's a park on the corner of 2nd Street and Maple in Springfield, but there isn't one in Riverside. There's a parking lot.
3.
4.
5.
6.
7.
8.
9.
10.

3 Answer these questions. Use the map and the prepositions in the box.

☐ across from	☐ between	☐ in
☐ near	☑ next to	☐ on the corner of

1. Where's the nearest bank?
   There's one next to the grocery store
   on 1st Avenue.
2. Is there a post office near here?
   Yes. There
3. I'm looking for a drugstore.
4. Is there a laundromat in this neighborhood?
5. Is there a department store on River Street?
6. Are there any ATMs around here?

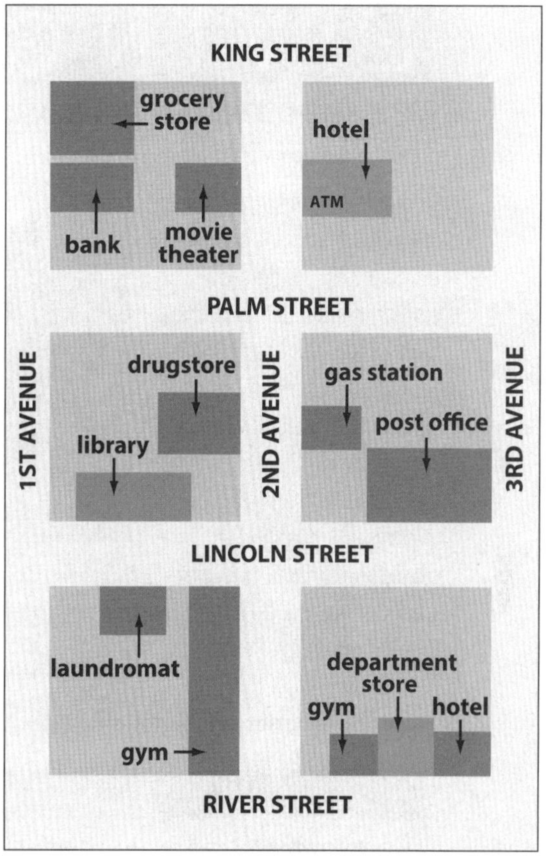

4 Answer these questions about your city or neighborhood. Use the expressions in the box and your own information.

Yes, there is. There's one on . . .	Yes, there are. There are some on . . .
No, there isn't.	No, there aren't.

1. Are there any good coffee shops around the school?
2. Is there a drugstore near the school?
3. Are there any grocery stores in your neighborhood?
4. Is there a laundromat close to your home?

5 The grass is always greener

A Read the interviews. Where would Charles like to live? Where would Arlene like to live?

HOME | STORIES | PHOTOS

MODERN LIVING

WE ASKED TWO PEOPLE ABOUT THE PLACES THEY LIVE.

Charles Bell

"My neighborhood is very convenient — it's near the shopping center and the bus station. It's also safe. But those are the only good things about living downtown. It's very noisy because the streets are always full of people! The traffic is terrible, and parking is a big problem! I can never park on my own street. I'd like to live in a small town."

Arlene Miller

"My family and I live in a nice small town. It has a great square where people meet for social events, and there's music on summer evenings. It's a safe place to raise children. But there is no privacy here. Everyone in town knows what you are doing all the time. And I don't meet as many interesting people as when I lived in the city. It can be too quiet here. I want more action! I think it's better downtown."

LIKE COMMENT

B How do Charles and Arlene feel about their neighborhoods? Complete the chart.

	Advantages	Disadvantages
Downtown	*convenient*	
Small Town		*no privacy*

C Do you think it's better to live downtown or in a small town? Why?

___

___

___

D How do you feel about the place you live? Write about it.

___

___

___

6 Complete the chart. Use words from the box.

☑ bank	☐ library	☐ people	☐ theater
☑ crime	☐ noise	☐ pollution	☐ traffic
☐ hospital	☐ parking	☐ school	☐ water

Count nouns		Noncount nouns	
bank		crime	

7 Write questions using *How much . . . ?* or *How many . . . ?* Then look at the picture and write answers to the questions. Use the expressions in the box.

☐ a few	☐ a lot	☐ many
☐ none	☐ not any	☑ only a little

1. trash How much trash is there? There's only a little.
2. buses ______ ______
3. traffic ______ ______
4. bicycles ______ ______
5. police officers ______ ______
6. crime ______ ______

8 Choose the correct words or phrases to complete the conversation.

Andrea: Are there ____any____ (any / one / none) coffee shops around here, Carlos?

Carlos: Sure. There are ____________ (any / one / a lot). There's a coffee shop ____________ (across from / between / on) the Daily Market, but it's expensive.

Andrea: Well, are there ____________ (any / none / one) others?

Carlos: Yeah, there are ____________ (a few / a little / one). There's a nice ____________ (any / one / some) near here. It's called Morning Joe.

Andrea: That's perfect! Where is it, exactly?

Carlos: It's on Third Avenue, ____________ (between / on / on the corner of) the National Bank and the Chinese restaurant.

Andrea: So let's go!

9 Choose the correct words or phrases.

1. I'm going to the grocery store to get some ____________________.
(clothes / gas / food)

2. We're taking a long drive. We need to stop at the ____________________.
(laundromat / gas station / drugstore)

3. I live on the 8th floor of my ____________________.
(apartment building / neighborhood / theater)

4. Our apartment is in the center of the city. We live ____________________.
(downtown / in the neighborhood / in the suburbs)

9 What does she look like?

1 Write the opposites. Use the words in the box.

☑ light ☐ straight ☐ young ☐ short ☐ tall

1. dark / light
2. curly / ______
3. short / ______
4. long / ______
5. elderly / ______

2 Descriptions

A Match the words in columns A and B. Write the descriptions.

A	B	
☑ medium	☐ aged	**1.** medium height
☐ fairly	☐ brown	**2.**
☐ good	☑ height	**3.**
☐ middle	☐ long	**4.**
☐ dark	☐ looking	**5.**

B Answer the questions using the descriptions from part A.

1. **A:** How tall is he?
   B: He's medium height.
2. **A:** What does he look like?
   B: ______
3. **A:** What color is his hair?
   B: ______
4. **A:** How long is his hair?
   B: ______
5. **A:** How old is he?
   B: ______

3 Complete this conversation with questions.

Marta: Let's find Arturo. I need to talk to him.

Alli: What does he look like?

Marta: He's very handsome, with curly brown hair.

Alli: And ______________________

Marta: It's medium length.

Alli: ______________________

Marta: He's fairly tall.

Alli: And ______________________

Marta: He's in his early twenties.

Alli: ______________________

Marta: Well, he usually wears jeans.

Alli: I think I see him over there. Is that him?

4 Describe yourself. How old are you? What do you look like? What are you wearing today?

____

____

____

____

____

5 Circle two things in each description that do not match the picture. Then correct the information.

Willie

1. Willie is a young man. He's pretty tall.
   He has a mustache and curly hair.
   He's wearing a jacket, jeans, and boots.
   He isn't young. He's . . . .

Sandy

2. Sandy is about 25. She's very pretty.
   She's medium height. Her hair is long and blond.
   She's wearing a black sweater, a skirt, and sneakers.

Anita

3. Anita is in her early thirties.
   She's pretty serious-looking. She has glasses.
   She's fairly tall, and has curly dark hair.
   She's wearing a nice-looking scarf and a skirt.

6 Which of these clothing items are more formal? Which are more casual? Complete the chart.

boots

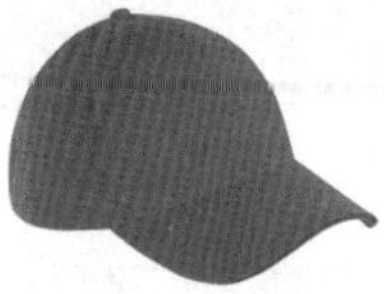
cap

dress

high heels

jeans

jewelry

necktie

shirt

Formal	Casual
dress	

shorts

sneakers

suit

T-shirt

7 Write a sentence about the people in the picture. Use the words in the box and participles.

- [x] man
- [ ] one
- [ ] ones
- [ ] short man
- [ ] young woman
- [ ] carry a jacket
- [ ] wear sunglasses
- [x] stand next to Angela
- [ ] talk to the man
- [ ] wear a suit and tie

1. Brad is the man standing next to Angela.
2. ______
3. ______
4. ______
5. ______

8 Write sentences about the people in the picture. Use the words given.

1. Charles and Natalie are the ones playing chess. (ones / playing chess)
2. ______________________________ (one / behind the couch)
3. ______________________________ (ones / eating pizza)
4. ______________________________ (woman / on the couch)
5. ______________________________ (man / short black hair)

9 Rewrite the conversations. Find another way to say the sentences using the words in the box.

☑ near	☐ sitting	☐ wearing	☑ which	☐ who	☐ who

1. **A:** Who's Lucas?
   Which one's Lucas?
   B: He's the guy next to the window.
   He's the guy near the window.
2. **A:** Which ones are the servers?
   ____
   B: They're the ones in the red polo shirts.
   ____
3. **A:** Which one is Naomi?
   ____
   B: She's the one on the couch next to Lisa.
   ____

10 Which one is Jeff?

Complete Bill and Ruby's conversation at a party. Use the present continuous or the participle of the verbs in the box.

☐ cook ☐ eat ☑ look ☐ play ☐ sit ☐ talk ☐ use ☐ wear

Ruby: I'm glad you brought me to this party, Bill. I'm ___looking___ for someone here named Jeff.

Bill: Yeah, I don't know too many people here. But let's try to find him. Is he one of those guys ________ football? What about the guy with black hair and ________ the dark T-shirt?

Ruby: Hmm, no. That's not Jeff.

Bill: How about the one ________ the music system over there, in the white T-shirt.

Ruby: No, I know him. That's Ken.

Bill: Hmm. Oh, is that Jeff ________ at the table and ________ to the two women? It looks like they're already ________.

Ruby: No, not him, either. Gee, I wonder if Jeff even came to the party?

Bill: Well, he can't be the chef, right? The guy ________ vegetables at the grill?

Ruby: That's him! Hey, Jeff!

11 Choose the correct responses.

1. **A:** Who's Shawn?
   B: The middle-aged man on the couch.
   - The middle-aged man on the couch.
   - That's right.

2. **A:** Where's Samantha?
   B: ________
   - She couldn't make it.
   - I'd like to meet her.

3. **A:** Is Avery the one wearing glasses?
   B: ________
   - That's right.
   - She's running late.

4. **A:** How tall is she?
   B: ________
   - Fairly long.
   - Pretty short.

10 Have you ever been there?

1 Match the verb forms in columns A and B.

A		B
1. make	g	a. tried
2. ride	___	b. eaten
3. do	___	c. seen
4. eat	___	d. had
5. go	___	e. ridden
6. have	___	f. heard
7. be	___	✓ g. made
8. hear	___	h. done
9. see	___	i. gone
10. try	___	j. been

2 Complete the questions in these conversations. Use the present perfect of the verbs in Exercise 1.

1. **A:** Have you seen Al's new dog?
   B: Yes, it's so cute!
2. **A:** How many times ______________ to the gym this month?
   B: Actually, not at all. Let's go later today!
3. **A:** How many phone calls ______________ today?
   B: I made two calls – both to you!
4. **A:** ______________ your homework yet?
   B: Yes, I have. I did it after class.
5. **A:** ______________ at the new Italian restaurant?
   B: Yes, we already have. It's very good but a little expensive.
6. **A:** How long ______________ those boots?
   B: I bought them on Monday.

3 *Already* and *yet*

A Check (✓) the things you've already done. Put an ✗ next to the things you haven't done yet.

1. ____ graduated from high school
2. ____ gotten married
3. ____ ridden a horse
4. ____ been in an airplane
5. ____ learned to drive
6. ____ traveled abroad

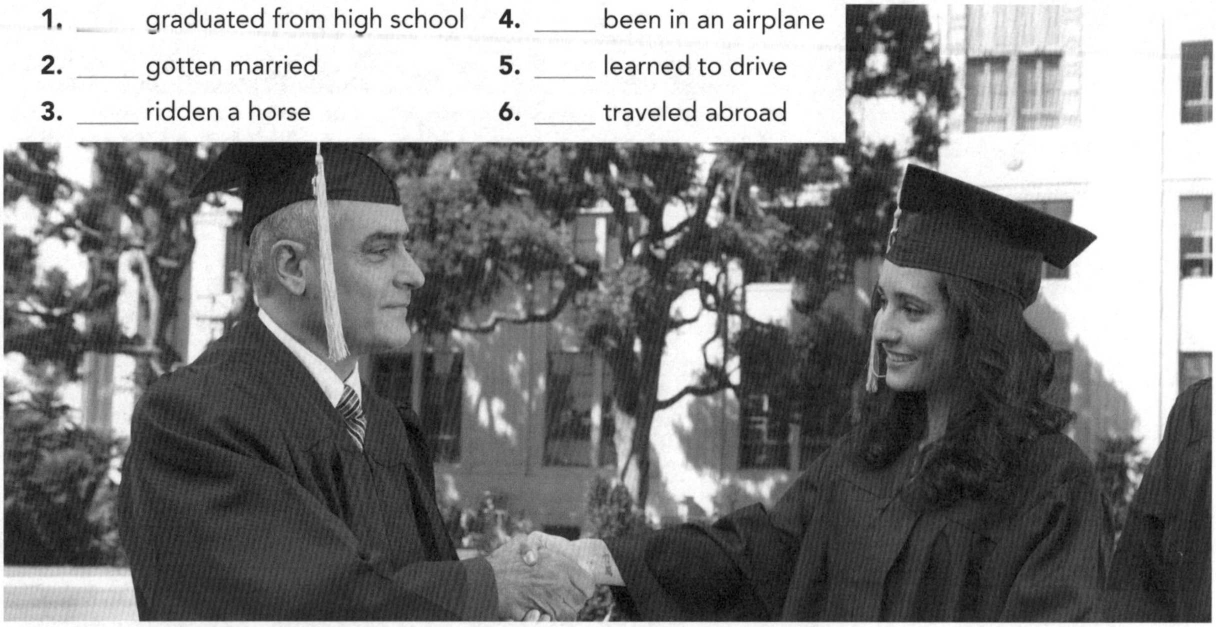

B Write sentences about each activity in part A. Use *already* and *yet*.

Grammar note: *Already* and *yet*

***Already* is used in positive statements with the present perfect.**
I've **already** graduated from high school.
***Yet* is used in negative statements with the present perfect.**
I haven't gotten married **yet**.

1. ____________________
2. ____________________
3. ____________________
4. ____________________
5. ____________________
6. ____________________

4 Complete these sentences with *for* or *since*.

1. Jill has driven the same car ____since____ 2004.
2. I have been a teacher ____________ several years.
3. I haven't had this much fun ____________ I was a kid!
4. I'm so sleepy. I've been awake ____________ 4:00 this morning.
5. Kyoko was an exchange student in Peru ____________ a whole semester.
6. Marcus has lived in Dubai ____________ 2010.
7. How are you? I haven't seen you ____________ high school.
8. Where have you been? I've been here ____________ over an hour!
9. Mr. and Mrs. Lopez have been married ____________ nearly 50 years.

5 Look at these pictures. How often have you done these things? Write sentences using the expressions in the box.

I've . . . many times.	I've . . . once or twice.
I've . . . three or four times.	I haven't . . . lately.
I've . . . several times.	I've never . . .

1. ______________________________

2. ______________________________

3. ______________________________

4. ______________________________

5. ______________________________

6. ______________________________

6 Lost tales

A Read the two blog posts. Where did each blogger go? What activity did each one want to do?

NO WAY OUT!

Have you ever visited Mexico? If so, then you know it is famous for its Aztec ruins. Last summer my Spanish class visited Mexico City. We went on a tour of Aztec ruins that are found under the city's main square. We walked for two hours underground in the dark halls. It was like being in a cave. There are many interesting things to see. I wanted to get a better look at a statue, so I went around some ropes that are supposed to keep tourists out. Several minutes later, I came out on the other side, but my group disappeared! I couldn't hear any voices, and I didn't know which way to go. I was too embarrassed to shout, so I wandered around the halls trying to find my group. I started to get nervous. It seemed like I was alone for hours. I walked around in the darkness until I finally heard the professor calling my name. He was very worried, and I was relieved! For the rest of our trip in Mexico, he made sure I never left his sight. My friends still call me "Cave Woman."

NO WAY IN!

I have been to Europe many times but never to Greece until last summer. It was an unforgettable experience! I was staying at a small hotel in Athens. It was in a part of town where most tourists don't stay, but it was cheaper there, and I wanted to practice speaking Greek with people. One evening I went for a walk before dinner. Soon it started to get dark. I didn't want to get lost, and I remembered I had a small map of Athens in my wallet. My wallet! It wasn't in my pocket. I thought, "I've left it in the hotel room . . . and my hotel key is in my wallet!" It took me a long time to get back to the hotel, but I made it. The door was locked, of course. Sometimes I talk to myself when I'm upset. Well, I must have said out loud, "I've lost my wallet, I've locked myself out, and I've missed dinner!" Just then, the hotel manager appeared. I guess he heard me talking. He said something in Greek and pointed to his house. I followed him. He and his family were having a big Greek dinner. They wanted me to join them. The manager eventually let me into my room. But first, I ate one of the best meals I've ever had. And forgetting my wallet was the best mistake I've ever made!

B In which story or stories did the writer(s) do these things? Write *1*, *2*, or *1 and 2*.

___1___ went to ruins
______ went to a foreign country
______ got lost
______ got help from someone
______ stayed at a hotel
______ went underground
______ made a mistake
______ went on the trip alone

C Write about an adventure you have had. What happened? What went wrong?

____
____
____
____

7 Look at the answers. Write questions using *Have you ever . . . ?*

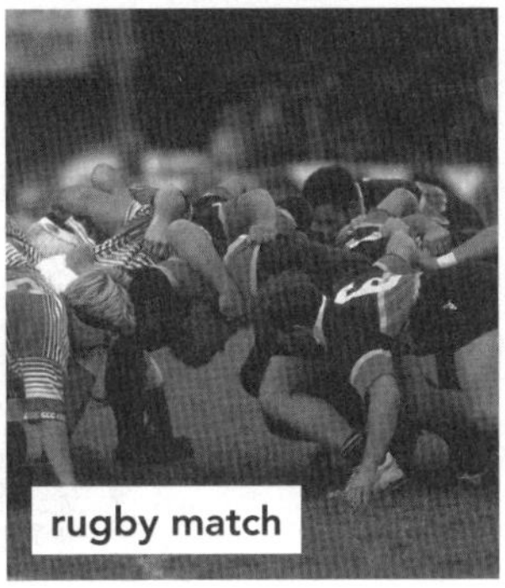

1. **A:** *Have you ever sent a text message during class?*
   B: No, I've never sent a text message during class.
2. **A:** ______________________________
   B: Actually, I saw a rugby match last week on TV. It was awesome!
3. **A:** ______________________________
   B: Yes, I love sushi.
4. **A:** ______________________________
   B: No, I haven't. But my uncle lives in Houston.
5. **A:** ______________________________
   B: Yes, I visited an amusement park last month.
6. **A:** ______________________________
   B: No, I haven't. I don't think I would like camping.
7. **A:** ______________________________
   B: Yes, I have. I once rode my aunt's motorcycle.

8 Write your own answers to the questions (speaker A) in Exercise 7. Use expressions like the ones from the list.

Yes, I have.	I . . . yesterday. I . . . on Monday. I . . . last year. I . . . in August.	No, I haven't.	I've never . . . I . . . yet.

1. ______________________________
2. ______________________________
3. ______________________________
4. ______________________________
5. ______________________________
6. ______________________________
7. ______________________________

9 Complete the conversation. Use the simple past or the present perfect of the words given.

A: ___Have___ you ever ___lost___ (lose) anything valuable?

B: Yes, I ________ (lose) my cell phone last month.

A: ________ you ________ (find) it yet?

B: No. Actually, I ________ already ________ (buy) a new one. Look!

A: Oh, that's nice. Where ________ you ________ (buy) it?

B: I ________ (get) it at the mall last weekend. What about you? ________ you ever ________ (lose) anything valuable?

A: Well, I ________ (leave) my leather jacket in a coffee shop a couple of months ago.

B: Oh, no! ________ you ________ (go) back and look for it?

A: Well, I ________ (call) them, but it was gone.

10 Choose the correct responses.

1. A: Has John visited his brother lately?
   B: ___No, he hasn't.___
   - How many times?
   - No, he hasn't.
2. A: Are you having a good time?
   B: ________
   - Yes, in a long time.
   - Yes, really good.
3. A: How long did Theresa stay at the party?
   B: ________
   - For two hours.
   - Since midnight.
4. A: Have you had breakfast?
   B: ________
   - Yes, in a few minutes.
   - Yes, I've already eaten.
5. A: How many times has Tony lost his keys?
   B: ________
   - Twice.
   - Not yet.
6. A: Do you want to see that new movie?
   B: ________
   - I never have. What about you?
   - Sure. I hear it's great.
7. A: Have you been here long?
   B: ________
   - No, not yet.
   - No, just a few minutes.
8. A: Have you seen Sara today?
   B: ________
   - Yes, I saw her this morning.
   - Yes, tomorrow.

11 It's a really nice city.

1 Choose the correct words to complete the sentences.

1. Prices are high in Singapore. Everything is very __expensive__ there.
(cheap / expensive / noisy)
2. Chicago has amazing skyscrapers right next to a gorgeous lake. It's a really ______________ city.
(beautiful / cheap / quiet)
3. My hometown is not an exciting place. The nightlife there is pretty ______________.
(boring / nice / interesting)
4. Some parts of our city are fairly dangerous. It's not very ______________ late at night.
(hot / interesting / safe)
5. The streets in this city are always full of people, cars, and buses. It's a very ______________ city.
(spacious / crowded / relaxing)

2 Choose the correct questions to complete this conversation.

- ☐ What's the weather like?
- ☐ Is it big?
- ☐ Is the nightlife exciting?
- ☑ What's your hometown like?

A: __What's your hometown like?__

B: My hometown? It's a pretty nice place, and the people are very friendly.

A: ______________________________

B: No, it's fairly small, but it's not too small.

A: ______________________________

B: The winter is wet and really cold. It's very nice in the summer, though.

A: ______________________________

B: No! It's really boring. There are no good restaurants or nightclubs.

3 Choose the correct conjunctions and rewrite the sentences.

Grammar note: *And, but, though,* and *however*

Use *and* for additional information.

It's an exciting city, **and** the weather is great.

Use *but, though,* and *however* for contrasting information.

It's very safe during the day, **but** it's pretty dangerous at night.

The summers are hot. The evenings are fairly cold, **though**.

It is a fairly large city. It's not too interesting, **however**.

Colorado

Dubai

Hong Kong

1. Colorado is beautiful in the summer. It's a great place to go hiking. (and / but)

   Colorado is beautiful in the summer, and it's a great place to go hiking.

2. Dubai is a very nice place. The summers are terribly hot. (and / though)

3. Hong Kong is an exciting city. It's a fun place to sightsee. (and / however)

4. My hometown has some great restaurants. It's not a good place for shopping. (and / but)

5. Our hometown is somewhat ugly. It has some beautiful old homes. (and / however)

4 Check (✓) if these sentences need *a* or *an*. Then write *a* or *an* in the correct places.

Grammar note: *A* and *an*

Use *a* or *an* with (adverb +) adjective + singular noun.
It has **a fairly new park**. It's **an old city**.
Don't use *a* or *an* with (adverb +) adjective.
It's **fairly new**. It's **old**.

1. ☑ London has ^a very famous Ferris wheel.
2. ☐ Restaurants are very cheap in Ecuador.
3. ☐ Brisbane is clean city.
4. ☐ The buildings in Florence are really beautiful.
5. ☐ Apartments are very expensive in Hong Kong.
6. ☐ Sapporo is very cold city in the winter.
7. ☐ Beijing's museums are really excellent.
8. ☐ Mumbai is exciting place to visit.

5 Complete the description of Paris with *is* or *has*.

PARIS: City of Light

Paris ______________ France's biggest city. It ______________ a very lively city with an interesting history. It ______________ a city of interesting buildings and churches, and it ______________ many beautiful parks. It also ______________ some of the best museums in the world. Paris ______________ nice weather most of the year, but it ______________ pretty cold in the winter. It ______________ a popular city with foreign tourists and ______________ millions of visitors a year. The city ______________ famous for its fashion and ______________ many excellent stores. Paris ______________ convenient trains and buses that cross the city, so it ______________ easy for tourists to get around.

6 From city to city

A Scan the webpage. Where is each city?

SEOUL

Seoul was founded in 18 BCE. It is South Korea's capital and today has a population of 10.5 million people. Seoul is famous for producing popular music and films that are very well known in Asia, Latin America, and the Middle East. The city is surrounded by mountains and located on the Han River. It has an excellent transportation system that can take you to 115 museums, monuments, parks, and music festivals throughout the city. The best time to visit Seoul is in the fall and the spring. Winters can be quite cold and summers very hot.

QUITO

Quito sits 2,850 meters above sea level and is the highest capital city in the world. Its population is 2.6 million people. The city is located near the equator in the country of Ecuador (which means "equator" in Spanish). Quito's downtown center, one of the most beautiful in the Americas, has not changed much since the Spanish founded the city in 1534. On a day trip from Quito, you can go walking in the mountains and visit a volcano there. Because of the city's elevation and location on the equator, the weather there is pleasant all year.

RABAT

Rabat is located on the Atlantic Ocean. It was founded in 1146. Although Rabat is the capital of Morocco, its population is only about 580,000 people. The weather is cool at night with hot days in the summer and mild days in the winter. Mawazine, a famous world music festival, takes place in Rabat in the spring. You can visit the Kasbah, an old fortress, and enjoy the architecture, gardens, and the view of the ocean. Rabat's outdoor markets sell beautiful handmade goods. Explore the city and enjoy a delicious Moroccan meal!

B Read the webpage and complete the chart.

City	Date founded	Population	Attractions
Seoul			
Quito			
Rabat			

C Complete the sentences.

1. ____________________ and ____________________ have music festivals.
2. ____________________ is the capital city with the smallest population.
3. ____________________ is the oldest capital city.
4. ____________________ has the capital city with the highest altitude.

7 Complete the sentences. Use phrases from the box.

☐ shouldn't miss	☐ can take
☑ should see	☐ shouldn't stay
☐ can get	☐ shouldn't walk

1. You ___should see___ the new zoo. It's very interesting.
2. You ________________ near the airport. It's too noisy.
3. You ________________ the museum. It has some new exhibits.
4. You ________________ a bus tour of the city if you like.
5. You ________________ alone at night. It's too dangerous.
6. You ________________ a taxi if you're out late.

8 Complete the conversation with *should* or *shouldn't* and *I* or *you*.

A: I'm taking my vacation in Japan. What ___should I___ do there?

B: ________________ miss Kyoto, the old capital city. There are a lot of beautiful old buildings. For example, ________________ see the Ryoanji Temple.

A: Sounds great. Hakone is very popular, too. ________________ go there?

B: Yes, ________________. It's very interesting, and the hot springs are fantastic.

A: ________________ take a lot of money with me?

B: No, ________________. You can use the ATMs in Japan.

A: So when ________________ go there?

B: In the spring or the fall. You can see the cherry blossoms or the fall colors.

9 Ask questions about a place you want to visit. Use *can, should,* or *shouldn't.*

1. the time to visit

   What time of year should I visit?

2. things to see and do there

   ____

3. things not to do

   ____

4. special foods to try

   ____

5. fun things to buy

   ____

6. other interesting things to do

   ____

10 Rewrite the sentences. Think of another way to express each sentence using the words given.

1. It's a polluted city.

   It isn't a clean city. (not clean)

2. You really should visit the new aquarium.

   ______________________________ (not miss)

3. Apartments are not cheap in my country.

   ______________________________ (extremely expensive)

4. This neighborhood is not noisy at all.

   ______________________________ (very quiet)

5. When should we visit the city?

   ______________________________ (a good time)

12 It's important to get rest.

1 Any suggestions?

A Check (✓) the best advice for each health problem.

1. a backache

- [x] use a heating pad
- [ ] get some exercise
- [ ] drink herbal tea

2. a bad cold

- [ ] see a dentist
- [ ] go to bed and rest
- [ ] go swimming

3. a burn

- [ ] take a multivitamin
- [ ] put it under cold water
- [ ] drink warm milk

4. a headache

- [ ] take some vitamin C
- [ ] take some pain medicine
- [ ] take a cough drop

5. an insect bite

- [ ] apply anti-itch cream
- [ ] use eyedrops
- [ ] drink lots of liquids

6. sore muscles

- [ ] drink lots of hot water
- [ ] take some cold medicine
- [ ] use some ointment

B Write a question about each problem in part A. Then write answers using the words from the box. Use the advice in part A or your own ideas.

It's important . . .	**It's sometimes helpful . . .**	**It's a good idea . . .**

1. A: *What should you do for a backache?*
B: *It's sometimes helpful to use a heating pad.*

2. A: ______________________________
B: ______________________________

3. A: ______________________________
B: ______________________________

4. A: ______________________________
B: ______________________________

5. A: ______________________________
B: ______________________________

6. A: ______________________________
B: ______________________________

2 Rewrite these sentences. Give advice using *it's important . . .*, *it's a good idea . . .*, or *it's sometimes helpful . . .* .

Grammar note: Negative infinitives

Problem	**Advice**	**Negative infinitive**
For the flu,	don't exercise a lot.	For the flu, it's a good idea **not to exercise** a lot.

1. For a toothache, don't eat cold foods.
   For a toothache, it's important not to eat cold foods.
2. For a sore throat, don't talk too much.
   ____
3. For a burn, don't put ice on it.
   ____
4. For insomnia, don't drink coffee at night.
   ____
5. For a fever, don't get out of bed.
   ____

3 Check (✓) three health problems you have had. Write what you did for each one. Use the remedies below or your own remedies.

Health problems

- ☐ a cough
- ☐ a headache
- ☐ insomnia
- ☐ a cold
- ☐ a backache
- ☐ the hiccups
- ☐ a sunburn
- ☐ stress

Some remedies

take some pain medicine
get some medicine from the drugstore
use some lotion
put some ointment on it
take some cough drops
see my doctor/dentist
go to bed
do nothing

Example: *Yesterday, I had a bad headache, so I took some pain medicine.*

1. ______________________________
2. ______________________________
3. ______________________________

4 Learning to laugh

A Scan the article. Check (✓) the sentence that is the better summary of the article.

☐ **People who laugh at least once a day live longer than people who don't.**
☐ **Laughter has important health benefits for your body.**

LAUGH IT OFF

Have you laughed today? If so, you probably did a good thing for your health.

Psychologists now consider laughing to be an important practice for good health. Laughter is known to reduce stress, improve the body's ability to fight disease, and make life happier and more interesting. It adds to the pleasure we get from other people and the enjoyment other people get from us.

Dr. Madan Kataria, the founder of Laughter Yoga, discovered that laughter does not have to be real to be good for the body. In Laughter Yoga, people combine yoga breathing with laughter exercises in a group. This allows people to practice laughing without the presence of humor. Dr. Kataria has found that the body responds well just to the physical act of laughing.

Dr. Annette Goodheart was one of the first doctors in the U.S. to promote laughter for health. In her book *Laughter Therapy: How to Laugh About Everything in Your Life That is Not Really Funny*, she writes, "Everyone usually knows what they think is funny or can laugh at. But I help people laugh about things that aren't funny and support them in re-balancing and resolving their pain."

People who say that laughter is the best medicine might be right. A laugh a day keeps the doctor away!

B Check (✓) True or False.

	True	False
1. Laughter can help the body fight disease.	☐	☐
2. The more you laugh, the more other people like you.	☐	☐
3. Laughter is healthier for you if it is real.	☐	☐
4. Psychologists believe it is healthy to laugh at all situations.	☐	☐
5. Dr. Goodheart helped patients focus only on funny things.	☐	☐

C Describe a time you laughed hard at something. How did you feel afterward?

____

____

____

5 What do you suggest?

A Complete the word map with medicines from the list.

- [ ] anti-itch cream
- [ ] bandages
- [ ] eyedrops
- [x] herbal tea
- [ ] insect spray
- [ ] muscle ointment
- [ ] pain medicine
- [ ] shaving cream

CONTAINERS

BOTTLE
______
______

BOX
herbal tea
______

TUBE
______
______

CAN
______
______

B What should these people buy? Give advice. Use the containers and medicine from part A.

1. Danielle is having trouble sleeping.
   She should buy a box of herbal tea.
2. Simon has a bad headache.
   ______
3. Maria's shoulders are sore after her workout.
   ______
4. There may be mosquitoes where Brenda's camping.
   ______
5. Sam has a cut on his hand.
   ______
6. Graciela has dry, itchy skin on her feet.
   ______
7. Nathan cut his chin when he shaved with soap and water.
   ______
8. Sally's eyes are red and itchy.
   ______

6 Check (✓) the correct sentences to make conversations.

1. **Pharmacist:** ☑ Can I help you?
   ☐ Should I help you?
   Customer: ☐ Yes. Can I have a bottle of pain medicine?
   ☐ Yes. I suggest a bottle of pain medicine.
   Pharmacist: Here you are.
   Customer: ☐ And what do you need for a sunburn?
   ☐ And what do you have for a sunburn?
   Pharmacist: ☐ Do you suggest this lotion?
   ☐ I suggest this lotion.
   Customer: Thanks.

2. **Pharmacist:** Hi. Can I help you?
   Customer: ☐ Yes. Can I suggest something for sore muscles?
   ☐ Yes. Could I have something for sore muscles?
   Pharmacist: ☐ Sure. Try this ointment.
   ☐ Sure. Could I try this ointment?
   Customer: ☐ Thanks. And what should you get for the flu?
   ☐ Thanks. And what do you suggest for the flu?
   Pharmacist: ☐ Can I have some of these tablets? They really work.
   ☐ Try some of these tablets. They really work.
   Customer: ☐ OK, thanks. I'll take them. And you should get a box of tissues.
   ☐ OK, thanks. I'll take them. And could I have a box of tissues?
   Pharmacist: Sure. Here you are.

7 Complete this conversation with the correct words.

A: Wow, you don't look very good! Do you feel OK?

B: No, I think I'm getting a cold. What should I do ____________ it?
(for / to / with)

A: You should stay ____________ home and go ____________ bed.
(at / in / of) (in / of / to)

B: You're probably right. I've got a really bad cough, too.

A: Try drinking some hot tea ____________ honey. It really helps.
(for / of / with)

B: Anything else?

A: Yeah, I suggest you get a big box ____________ tissues!
(at / in / of)

8 Give suggestions for these problems. Use words from the box.

Try . . .	I suggest . . .	You should . . .

1. I can't stop sneezing.
   Try some allergy medicine.
2. I have a stomachache.
   ____
3. I don't have any energy.
   ____
4. I think I'm getting a cold.
   ____
5. I'm stressed out!
   ____
6. I have a very sore throat.
   ____

13 What would you like?

1 Show that you agree. Write sentences with the words given.

1. **A:** I don't want fast food tonight.
   B: I don't either. (either)

2. **A:** I really like Mexican food.
   B: ________________ (so)

3. **A:** I'm in the mood for Italian food.
   B: ________________ (too)

4. **A:** I can't stand spicy food.
   B: ________________ (neither)

5. **A:** I don't like greasy food very much.
   B: ________________ (either)

6. **A:** I want to eat healthy food for lunch.
   B: ________________ (too)

2 What do you think?

A Look at the pictures. Write sentences about the food. Use the expressions in the box and the given words.

Useful expressions

I love . . .	I'm crazy about . . .
I can't stand . . .	I'm not crazy about . . .
I don't like . . . very much.	It's a little too . . .
I like . . . a lot.	

1. It's a little too greasy.

2. ______________________

3. ______________________

4. ______________________

5. ______________________

B What are three of your favorite kinds of food? Write what you like about them.

____

____

____

____

3 To your taste

A Skim the restaurant reviews. Match the reviewer with the number of stars.

1. Carlota	★	Awful!
2. Adam	★★★	Pretty good.
3. Luka	★★★★★	Fantastic!!

YUM! Restaurant Reviews

Find a restaurant ...

QUINOA CORNER

175 PLEASANT ST.

Carlota

Quinoa Corner is my latest discovery! This international food restaurant has everything: delicious steak, hamburgers, Mexican enchiladas, Mediterranean salads, and vegetarian and vegan dishes, too. When I was there last Saturday, I ordered a grilled salmon with baby asparagus and a baked potato. Delicious! And the atmosphere is wonderful. The servers are dressed as cowboys and cowgirls. Every hour they do a square dance and sing a song for the diners. I love this place!

Luka

Last Sunday I took my wife to Quinoa Corner. I had sushi with rice and a cucumber salad. My wife had lamb curry with spicy vegetables and garlic bread. For dessert we both had chocolate cake. The sushi was quite good, although the salad was not as fresh as I'd like. My wife said that her curry was delicious, but that the vegetables were a little too salty. And I thought the servers were kind of silly. Despite those problems, we still recommend this restaurant.

Adam

For dinner last Thursday, I visited Quinoa Corner for the first time. I ordered the quinoa burger and an almond milkshake. They served me a real hamburger! While I was trying to explain the mistake to my server, she stepped away and began to dance and sing with the other "cowboys"! It took another half hour before my quinoa burger got to the table. When it did, it was cold, bland, and greasy! I do not recommend this restaurant.

B Read the reviews and complete the chart.

	Carlota	Luka	Luka's wife	Adam
Ordered:				
Problems:	☐ yes ☐ no	☐ yes ☐ no	☐ yes ☐ no	☐ yes ☐ no
Recommends:	☐ yes ☐ no	☐ yes ☐ no	☐ yes ☐ no	☐ yes ☐ no

4 Check (✓) the item that does not belong in each group.

1. ☐ apples
   ☑ broccoli
   ☐ strawberries

2. ☐ sushi
   ☐ pasta
   ☐ bread

3. ☐ ice cream
   ☐ iced coffee
   ☐ iced tea

4. ☐ corn
   ☐ green beans
   ☐ pork

5. ☐ beef
   ☐ bread
   ☐ chicken

6. ☐ a cookie
   ☐ a turkey sandwich
   ☐ a hamburger

5 Use one or more words to complete this conversation between a server and a customer.

Server: May I take your order?

Customer: ___Yes, I'll have___ the salmon.

Server: What kind of dressing ________________ on your salad – French, blue cheese, or vinaigrette?

Customer: ________________ like French, please.

Server: And would you like ________________ to drink?

Customer: Yes, ________________ have iced coffee.

Server: With milk and sugar?

Customer: Yes, ________________.

Server: Anything else?

Customer: No, ________________. That'll ________________ all.

6 Choose the correct responses.

1. **A:** What would you like?
   B: I'll have a beef burrito.
   - I'll be your server today.
   - Yes, I'd like to.
   - I'll have a beef burrito.
2. **A:** Would you like soup or salad?
   B: ______________________
   - I guess I will, thanks.
   - I'd like soup, please.
   - Yes, please.
3. **A:** What would you like on your pizza?
   B: ______________________
   - I'll have pepperoni.
   - I'd like a soda, please.
   - Small, please.
4. **A:** Would you like anything to drink?
   B: ______________________
   - No, thanks.
   - Yes, a hamburger, please.
   - I'll have some noodles, please.
5. **A:** What flavor ice cream would you like?
   B: ______________________
   - Fresh, please.
   - Vanilla, please.
   - Ice cream, please.
6. **A:** Would you like anything else?
   B: ______________________
   - Yes, thank you very much.
   - Not at all, thanks.
   - That'll be all, thanks.

7 Choose the correct words.

1. Baked potatoes are less greasy than french fries. (greasy / healthy / spicy)
2. In a restaurant, the server takes your ______________. (table / order / service)
3. Many people like ______________ on their salad. (dessert / dressing / soda)
4. Some people rarely cook with spices. They prefer food to be ______________. (bland / hot / rich)
5. Strawberry is a popular ice cream ______________. (drink / flavor / meal)

8 Complete the conversation. Use the words and expressions in the box.

☐ am	☐ favorite kind of food	☐ too
☐ can	☐ like it a lot	☐ I'll
☐ can't stand them	☑ neither	☐ would
☐ do	☐ so	

Maria: I feel tired tonight. I really don't want to cook.

Courtney: ___Neither___ do I. Let's order out. Do you like Chinese food?

Maria: It's delicious! I ______________________!

Courtney: I do, ______________________. It's my ______________________.
Let's call Beijing Express for home delivery.

Maria: Great idea! Their food is always good. I eat there a lot.

Courtney: ______________________ do I. Well, what ______________________ you like tonight?

Maria: I'm in the mood for some soup.

Courtney: So ______________________ I. And I think ______________________ have orange chicken and fried rice.

Maria: OK, let's order. Oh, wait. They don't take credit cards, and I don't have any cash on me.

Courtney: Neither ______________________ I. Too bad! What should we do?

Maria: Well, let's look in the refrigerator. Hmm. Do you like boiled eggs?

Courtney: I ______________________!

Maria: Actually, neither ______________________ I.

14 It's the coldest city!

1 Geography

A Circle the correct word.

1. This is a mountain with a hole on top. Smoke and lava sometimes come out, and it can be dangerous.

a. waterfall **b.** volcano **c.** hill

2. This is a dry, sandy place. It doesn't rain much here, and there aren't many plants.

a. desert **b.** sea **c.** volcano

3. This is a low area of land between mountains or hills.

a. island **b.** valley **c.** beach

4. This is an area of water with land all around it.

a. hill **b.** island **c.** lake

5. This is a flow of water that happens when a river falls from a high place.

a. hill **b.** canyon **c.** waterfall

6. This is a large area of land that has lots of trees on it.

a. desert **b.** forest **c.** river

B Complete the names. Use words from the box.

☐ Canyon	☐ Falls	☐ Ocean	☑ Lake
☐ Desert	☐ Mount	☐ River	☐ Sea

1. ___Lake___ Superior

2. Amazon ______________

3. Grand ______________

4. Atlantic ______________

5. Mojave ______________

6. Niagara ______________

7. Mediterranean ______________

8. ______________ Everest

2 Write the comparative and superlative forms of the words given.

Spelling note: Comparatives and superlatives

	Adjective	Comparative	Superlative
Add *-er* or *-est* to most words.	long	long**er**	the long**est**
Add *-r* or *-st* to words ending in *-e*.	large	large**r**	the large**st**
Drop the y and add *-ier* or *-iest*.	dry	dr**ier**	the dr**iest**
Double the final consonant and add *-er* or *-est*.	big	bi**gger**	the bi**ggest**

1. busy ___busier___ ___the busiest___
2. cool ________ ________
3. friendly ________ ________
4. heavy ________ ________
5. nice ________ ________
6. noisy ________ ________
7. old ________ ________
8. safe ________ ________
9. small ________ ________
10. wet ________ ________

3 Complete this conversation. Use the superlative form of the words given.

Keegan: So where did you go for your vacation, Kathy?

Kathy: Japan.

Keegan: How exciting! Did you have a good time?

Kathy: It was terrific! I think Japan is ___the most exciting___ (exciting) country in Asia.

Keegan: Well, it certainly has some of ________ (interesting) cities in the world – Tokyo, Osaka, and Kyoto.

Kathy: Yeah. I had ________ (good) time in Kyoto. It's ________ (beautiful) city I've ever seen. Of course, it's also one of ________ (popular) tourist attractions. It was ________ (crowded) city I visited this summer.

Keegan: I've always wanted to visit Japan. What's it like in the winter?

Kathy: Actually, I think that's ________ (bad) time to visit because I don't like cold weather. However, I think the Sapporo Snow Festival is ________ (fascinating) festival in the world.

4 Complete these sentences. Use the comparative or the superlative form of the words given.

Badwater Basin

the Suez Canal

Mount Waialeale

1. Badwater Basin in California's Death Valley is ___the lowest___ (low) point in North America.
2. The Suez Canal joins the Mediterranean and Red Seas. It is 190 kilometers (118 miles) long. It is ___longer than___ (long) the Panama Canal.
3. Mount Waialeale in Hawaii gets 1,170 centimeters (460 inches) of rain a year. It is ______________ (wet) place on Earth!
4. Canada and Russia are ______________ (large) countries in the world.
5. Russia is ______________ (large) Canada.
6. ______________ (high) waterfall in the world is in Venezuela.
7. The Atacama Desert in Chile is ______________ (dry) place in the world.
8. ______________ (hot) capital city in the world is Muscat, Oman.
9. The continent of Antarctica is ______________ (cold) any other place in the world.
10. The Himalayas are some of ______________ (dangerous) mountains to climb.
11. Mont Blanc in the French Alps is ______________ (high) the Matterhorn in the Swiss Alps.
12. The Pacific Ocean is ______________ (deep) the Atlantic Ocean. At one place, the Pacific Ocean is 11,033 meters (36,198 feet) deep.

5 The coldest and the windiest!

A Scan the article about Antarctica. In what ways is it different from other places on Earth? Why do scientists work there?

ANTARCTICA is the most southern continent in the world. It's like nowhere else on Earth. It's much larger than Europe and nearly twice the size of Australia. It's an icy plateau with the South Pole at its center. Antarctica is the coldest and windiest place in the world, even colder and windier than the North Pole. Although 98 percent of Antarctica is covered in ice, it is considered a desert. Along the coast, annual precipitation is only 200 millimeters (eight inches) a year. Very few plants grow there, but there is some wildlife, including whales, seals, and penguins. In the summer, the sun shines for 24 hours a day, but in the winter, it's completely dark for about three months.

When Captain James Cook sailed around the continent in the 1770s, he found no one living there. Today, a few scientists work in Antarctica, but they only spend fairly short periods of time there. Many of these scientists live and work on the Antarctic Peninsula. This area is the closest part of Antarctica to South America, the continent's nearest neighbor. Many of these scientists are studying the effects of climate change there.

Antarctica has warmed by about 2.5 degrees Celsius since 1950. Some ice is melting in certain parts of the continent. However, unlike the vast melting that is happening in the Arctic, the ice in Antarctica is actually growing in spite of global warming.

Scientists think that this cold and lonely place can teach us a lot about the earth and how to keep it safe.

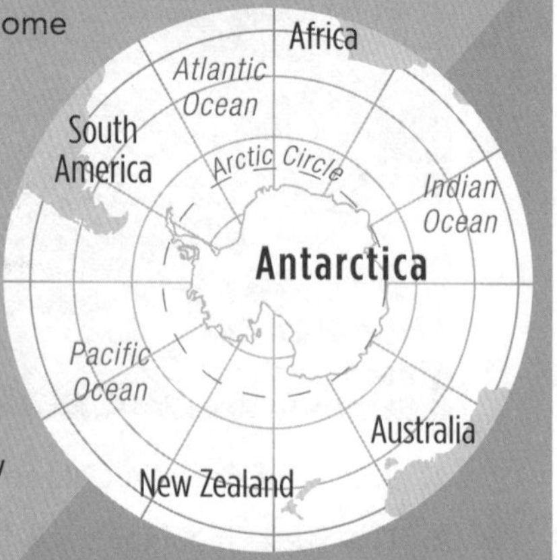

B Read about Antarctica. Check (✓) True or False.

	True	False
1. Antarctica is bigger than Europe.	☐	☐
2. The North Pole is the coldest place in the world.	☐	☐
3. The coasts in Antarctica get a lot of snow.	☐	☐
4. In Antarctica, it never gets dark in the summer.	☐	☐
5. Captain Cook discovered a few people living in Antarctica.	☐	☐
6. The Antarctic Peninsula is the closest part of Antarctica to South America.	☐	☐
7. Ice in Antarctica is melting throughout the continent.	☐	☐

6 Geography quiz

Use the words in the box. Write questions about the pictures. Then circle the correct answers.

- [ ] How big
- [ ] How cold
- [ ] How deep
- [ ] How far
- [ ] How long
- [x] How high

Angel Falls

1. How high is Angel Falls?
   a. It's 979 meters (3,212 feet) tall.
   (b.) It's 979 meters high.

2. ______________________________
   a. It's 6,300 kilometers (3,917 miles) long.
   b. It's 6,300 kilometers high.

the Yangtze River

Antarctica

3. ______________________________
   a. It gets up to –88.3 degrees Celsius (–126.9 degrees Fahrenheit).
   b. It gets down to –88.3 degrees Celsius.

4. ______________________________
   a. It's about 2,000 kilometers (1,200 miles).
   b. It's about 2,000 square kilometers.

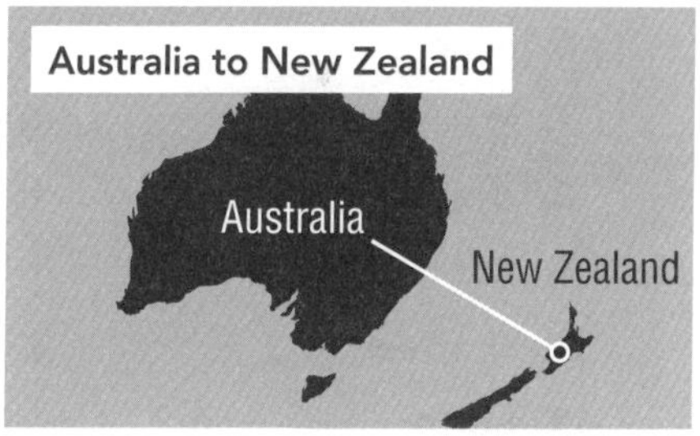

Australia to New Zealand

the Amazon Rain Forest

5. ______________________________
   a. It's 6 million square kilometers (2.5 million square miles).
   b. It's 6 million kilometers long.

6. ______________________________
   a. It's about 1.6 kilometers (1 mile) big.
   b. It's about 1.6 kilometers deep.

the Grand Canyon

7 Answer these questions about your country.

1. How big is the largest city?

______

2. What's the wettest month?

______

3. What's the driest month?

______

4. How hot does it get in the summer?

______

5. How cold does it get in the winter?

______

6. How high is the highest mountain?

______

7. What's the most beautiful town to visit?

______

8 Match the words with their opposites.

1. biggest	f	a. better
2. bad	____	b. wettest
3. shorter	____	c. colder
4. worse	____	d. drier
5. worst	____	e. hottest
6. near	____	f. smallest
7. lowest	____	g. far
8. driest	____	h. bigger
9. hot	____	i. good
10. shortest	____	j. best
11. hotter	____	k. low
12. smaller	____	l. highest
13. coldest	____	m. longest
14. wetter	____	n. wet
15. dry	____	o. taller
16. high	____	p. cold

15 What are you doing later?

1 Match the words in columns A and B. Write the names of the events.

A	B	
☑ baseball	☐ appointment	1. *baseball game*
☐ birthday	☐ concert	2.
☐ car	☑ game	3.
☐ class	☐ match	4.
☐ medical	☐ party	5.
☐ rock	☐ race	6.
☐ tennis	☐ reunion	7.

2 Read Joe's calendar and write about his plans each day. Use be going to.

Calendar

Day | Week | Month | Year

March

< This week >

Sunday	Monday	Tuesday	Wednesday	Thursday	Friday	Saturday
4	5	6	7	8	9	10
afternoon – play tennis with Brock	attend the managers' meeting at work	6:00 p.m. – see a movie with Angela	night – watch the soccer match with Annie and Bob	noon – have lunch with Paco	evening – go to the rock concert with friends	stay home and do laundry

1. *On Sunday afternoon, Joe is going to play tennis with Brock.*
2. ______________________
3. ______________________
4. ______________________
5. ______________________
6. ______________________
7. ______________________

3 Complete this conversation. Use *be going to* and the verbs given.

Stacey: What ____are____ you ____going to do____ this weekend, Hannah? (do)

Hannah: I ________________ to a jazz concert on Saturday. (go)

Stacey: That sounds interesting.

Hannah: Yeah. There's a free concert in the park. What about you, Stacey?

Stacey: Well, Ryan and I ________________ a baseball game in the afternoon. (see)

Hannah: And what __________ you ________________ in the evening? (do)

Stacey: Ryan ________________ his mother in the hospital. (visit) But I __________ not ________________ anything really. (do)

Hannah: Well, I ________________ some friends over for a barbecue. (have) Would you like to come?

Stacey: Thanks, I'd love to!

4 Choose the correct responses.

1. **A:** There's a basketball game on TV tonight. Do you want to watch it?

   B: ____I'm sorry. I'm working late tonight.____
   - How about this evening?
   - I'm sorry. I'm working late tonight.
   - Yes, it does.

2. **A:** Would you like to have dinner at Bella's Bistro tonight?

   B: ________________________________
   - No, I'm not doing anything.
   - Sorry, I'm going away next week.
   - Yes, that sounds great! But it's my turn to pay.

3. **A:** Do you want to go hiking tomorrow?

   B: ________________________________
   - Yes, I'm going to.
   - Can we go to a late show?
   - Sure, I'd love to.

4. **A:** How about going to a movie on Saturday?

   B: ________________________________
   - Oh, I'm sorry. I can't.
   - Nothing special.
   - No, I wouldn't.

5 Write invitations to this week's events in Eagleton.

Exciting things to do this week in **EAGLETON!**

MONDAY	TUESDAY	WEDNESDAY	THURSDAY
Pop concert Ellie Goulding	**Summer Festival** Lots to do for everyone!	**Musical** Jersey Boys	**Museum** Modern art exhibition opening

1. *Are you doing anything on Monday evening? Do you want to see a pop concert?* OR
   I'm going to go to the Ellie Goulding concert on Monday. Would you like to come?
2. ______________________________
3. ______________________________
4. ______________________________

6 Write about how often you do these leisure activities. Use the expressions in the box.

> I . . . almost every weekend.
> I never . . .
> I often . . .
> I sometimes . . . in the summer.
> I . . . three or four times a year.

1. ______________________________
2. ______________________________
3. ______________________________
4. ______________________________
5. ______________________________
6. ______________________________

1

go to the park

2

go to concerts

3

have parties at home

4

see plays

5

watch horror movies

6

go on picnics

7 I need help!

A Read Hannah's social media post and the comments from her friends. Why does she need help?

Wall | Find friends | Chat   Profile | Sign out

Hannah   1h ago

Guess what? I'm moving! Is anyone around Saturday morning and (maybe?) afternoon to help me move things to my new apartment? I only have a few heavy things, but I could use all the help I can get. I'll provide pizza for dinner! Tell your friends and let me know!

Pablo   58 minutes ago

Cool, where are you moving? I wish I could help you Saturday, but I'm going to the beach. Don't hate me. I'm available on Sunday . . . but that probably doesn't help you. Sorry!

Richard   55 minutes ago

Congratulations on the new place! I can help, but not until the afternoon. My study group is getting together to prepare for the chemistry exam on Monday (yikes!). See you after lunch?

Lien   50 minutes ago

Whoo-hoo, new apartment! Saturday morning I have to go to my little brother's baseball tournament. But I'll come over right after it's finished. What's the address?

Kalil   42 minutes ago

I'm so sorry, Hannah. I'm going to be working all weekend. I know, bummer. Can't wait to visit, though. Save me a slice of pizza! I like leftovers. ;-)

Rachel   30 minutes ago

I can't wait to see your new apartment! I'm going to visit my grandmother all day, so unfortunately I can't come until the evening – probably when the pizza arrives! Hope that's OK . . .

Eliana   24 minutes ago

Oh, bad timing! I have the city bicycle race on Saturday morning. But I can come when it's over. In fact, I'm going to keep riding past the finish line and straight to your place! See you in the afternoon.

Daichi   15 minutes ago

Pizza?! I'm in. But wait. I need to drive my sister to her dance class and then to her basketball game. Argh. Can she move in with you? Just kidding. I'll be there by 3:00.

B Match Hannah's friends with their reasons for not being able to help her or for showing up to help late.

1. _____ has a bicycle race.   **a.** Daichi
2. _____ has to study.   **b.** Eliana
3. _____ has to drive his sister around.   **c.** Kalil
4. _____ is going to the beach.   **d.** Pablo
5. _____ is going to work all weekend.   **e.** Rachel
6. _____ is going to a baseball tournament.   **f.** Richard
7. _____ is going to visit her grandmother.   **g.** Lien

8 Read these messages. What did the caller say? Write the messages another way using *tell* or *ask*.

For: *Mr. Jones*

Message: *The meeting is at 10:30. Arrive 10 minutes early.*

1. Please tell Mr. Jones that the meeting is at 10:30.
   Could you ask him to arrive 10 minutes early?

For: *Ms. Rodriguez*

Message: *We need the report by noon. Call Ms. Brady as soon as possible.*

2. ______________________________
   ____

For: Mr. Welch

Message: The new laptop is ready. Pick it up this afternoon.

3. ______________________________
   ____

9 Look at the text messages. Write sentences asking someone to give these messages.

Grammar note: Negative infinitives

Request	**Message**
Don't call him today.	Please ask Jan **not to call** him today.
Don't go home yet.	Could you tell him **not to go** home yet?

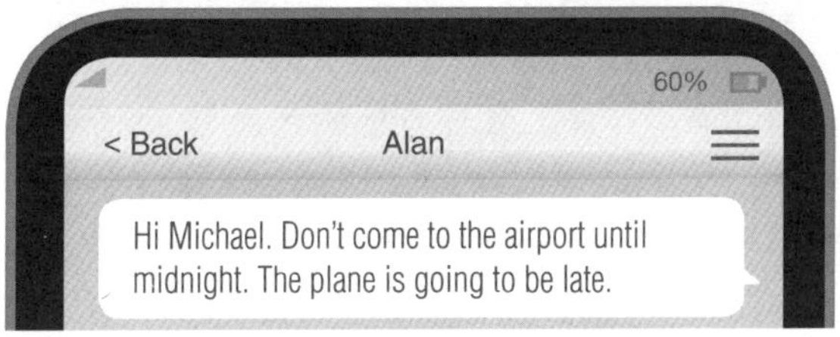

1. ______________________________
   ____
   ____

2. ______________________________
   ____
   ____

3. ______________________________
   ____
   ____

10 Choose the correct words.

Receptionist: Hello. McKenzie Corporation.

Mr. Brown: ___May I___ speak to Mr. Scott Myers, please?
(May I / Would you)

Receptionist: I'm ______________. He's not in. ______________ a message?
(busy / sorry) (Can I leave / Can I take)

Mr. Brown: Yes, please. This is Mr. Brown. ______________ you ______________
(Would / Please) (tell him that / ask him to)

I have to reschedule our meeting? My phone number is 303-555-9001.

______________ you ______________?
(Please / Could) (ask him to call me / ask me to call him)

Receptionist: OK, Mr. Brown. I'll ______________ the message.
(give him / tell him)

Mr. Brown: Thank you very much. Good-bye.

11 Match the questions with the correct responses.

- [ ] Let me see if she's in.
- [ ] This is John. John Abrams.
- [ ] Oh, no. I don't eat meat.
- [x] That's OK. I'll call back.
- [ ] Sure, I'd love to come. Thanks.
- [ ] Yes. My number is 303-555-3241.

1. I'm sorry. She's busy at the moment.
   ___That's OK. I'll call back.___
2. Could I ask her to call you back?
   ____
3. Who's calling, please?
   ____
4. Would you like to come to a party?
   ____
5. Could I speak to Tiffany, please?
   ____
6. Why don't we eat at Sam's Steakhouse tonight?
   ____

16 How have you changed?

1 Choose the correct responses.

1. **A:** Hey, you really look different.
   B: Well, I've grown a mustache.
   - I moved into a new house.
   - I'm more outgoing than before.
   - Well, I've grown a mustache.
2. **A:** I haven't seen you for ages.
   B: ______________________________
   - I know. How have you been?
   - Well, I got a bank loan.
   - My new job is more stressful.
3. **A:** You know, I have three kids now.
   B: ______________________________
   - No, I haven't graduated from college yet.
   - Wow, I can't believe it!
   - Say, you've really changed your hair.
4. **A:** How are you?
   B: ______________________________
   - I hope to get my driver's license soon.
   - Well, actually, I turned 18.
   - I'm doing really well.

2 Complete the sentences. Use information in the box and the present perfect.

☐ fall in love	☐ get two pay raises	☐ start an online course

1. JoAnn ______________________________ this year. Now she has enough money to buy a house.
2. Irvin ______________________________. He's studying to become a graphic designer.
3. Gisela and Russ ______________________________. They're going to get married in December.

3 Describe how these people have changed. Use the present or the past tense.

1. Mr. and Mrs. Kim had a baby.

2. Sara ______________________.

3. Ella ______________________.

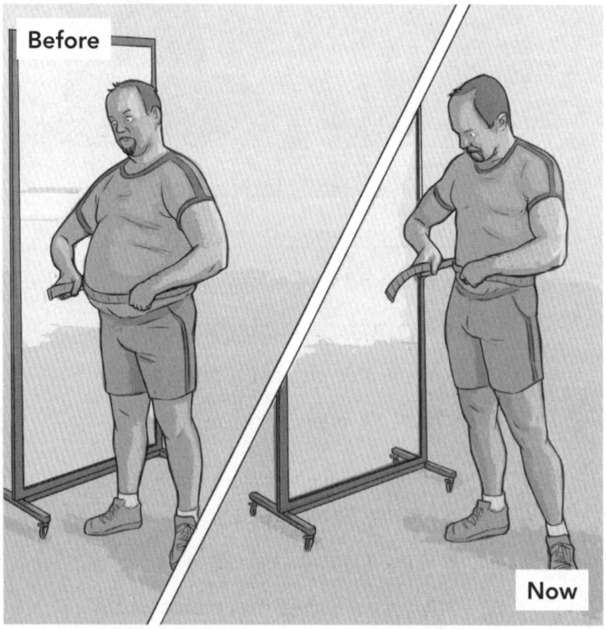

4. Ron ______________________.

4 Rewrite these sentences. Find another way to say each sentence using the words given.

1. I've grown out my hair.
   My hair is longer now. (longer)
2. Raquel gained a lot of weight.
   ______________________ (heavier)
3. Ben goes to a new school now.
   ______________________ (change)
4. Helen and George got divorced last year.
   ______________________ (married)
5. Traci quit eating fast food.
   ______________________ (healthier)
6. We quit working out at the gym.
   ______________________ (not go)

5 Life changes

A Read the passages on the left in part B. Complete these sentences.

1. ______________________ had an interesting job two years ago.
2. ______________________ had money problems two years ago.
3. ______________________ was a student two years ago.

B Now read the passages on the right. Match the people's lives two years ago with their lives now.

Two years ago	Now
1. **Rafael** Two years ago, I was a student, and I thought life was really good. I got up late. I spent the day talking to friends, and then I studied all night. I wore jeans and sweatshirts and had long hair and a beard. I felt free. _____	a. Now my life has completely changed. I got married six months ago! My husband and I often have friends over for dinner. We're taking classes several nights a week. It's great! We're even talking about starting a family soon.
2. **Diane** I moved to a new town two years ago. My job was interesting, but I was single and I didn't have any friends. People at work were friendly but not very outgoing. We never did anything after work. _____	b. Now I work as a computer programmer for an international company. I've moved to Seoul and have started to learn Korean. Korean food is great, and I've gained a few pounds. I feel much happier and healthier.
3. **Krystina** My life seemed to come to an end two years ago. I lost my job. Then I lost weight and looked terrible. Money became a problem. I was very sad. I needed some good luck. _____	c. Now I actually look forward to getting up early in the morning and going to work. Of course, I dress up now, and my hair is shorter. But I don't really mind. At least my evenings are free!

C Underline at least two changes in each person's life.

6 Complete the sentences. Use the words in the box.

☐ broke	☐ graduation	☐ responsibilities
☐ career	☑ loan	☐ successful

1. Rhonda wants to pay off her student ___loan___ before she buys a car.
2. I'd like to be ______________ in my first job. Then I can get a better job and a raise.
3. I go to school, and I have a family and a part-time job. I have a lot of ______________.
4. After ______________, Amelia and Lee plan to look for jobs.
5. Max lost his job. Now he's ______________, and he can't pay his rent.
6. What ______________ are you most interested in pursuing?

7 Complete this conversation. Use the words given.

Mariko: What ___do you plan to do___ (plan, do) this summer, Brian?

Brian: I ______________________ (want, get) a summer job. I ______________________ (like, save) money for a vacation.

Mariko: Really? Where ______________________ (like, go)?

Brian: I ______________________ (love, travel) to Latin America. What about you, Mariko?

Mariko: Well, I ______________________ (not go, get) a job right away. First, I ______________________ (want, go) to Spain and Portugal.

Brian: Sounds great, but how ______________________ (go, pay) for it?

Mariko: I ______________________ (hope, borrow) some money from my brother. I have a good excuse. I ______________________ (plan, take) courses in Spanish and Portuguese.

Brian: Oh, I'm tired of studying!

Mariko: I love to study. I also ______________________ (hope, take) people on tours to Latin America. Why don't you come on my first tour?

Brian: Count me in!

8 Imagine you have these problems. Write three sentences about changing your situation. Use the words in the box.

1. I just moved to a new town, and I don't know anyone. I never do anything after work. People at work don't really talk to me. I haven't had a date in about four months. And I never find anything fun to do on the weekends.

I'm going to . . .	I want to . . .	I plan to . . .

____
____
____
____
____

2. I've become less careful about my health lately. I've stopped jogging because I'm bored with it. I've started eating more fast food because I'm too tired to cook after work. And I can't sleep at night.

I'm going to . . .	I'd like to . . .	I'd love to . . .

____
____
____
____
____

3. My job is so boring. I spend two hours driving to and from work every day, and I don't make enough money! I can't find a new job, though, because of my poor computer skills.

I hope to . . .	I want to . . .	I plan to . . .

____
____
____
____
____

9 Choose the correct words to complete each sentence. Use the correct form of the word and add any words if necessary.

1. Floyd hopes to ___move___ to a small town.
(move / live / change)

2. This job is ____________________ my last job.
(outgoing / stressful / crowded)

3. After graduation, Kira plans ____________________ for an international company.
(play / work / move)

4. Stephanie's salary is much ____________________ before. She had to take a pay cut.
(low / short / high)

5. I hope to buy a house soon. I need ____________________ a bank loan.
(open / start / get)

6. Neil and Kelly got ____________________ last summer. The wedding will be in April.
(engage / marry)

10 Advise people how to make changes in their lives. Use expressions like the ones in the box.

Why don't you . . .	**You should . . .**	**You shouldn't . . .**

1. I've gained a lot of weight this year.
____

2. My hair is longer, but it doesn't look good.
____

3. I've gotten tired of wearing the same old clothes.
____

4. I want to start a successful business.
____

5. I'm often bored on weekends.
____

6. I don't really have any goals.
____

7. I've finished this textbook, but I still want to improve my English!
____